Equine Fitness

A CONDITIONING PROGRAM
of Exercises & Routines for Your Horse

JEC ARISTOTLE BALLOU

Storey Publishing

The mission of Storey Publishing is to serve our customers by
publishing practical information that encourages
personal independence in harmony with the environment.

Edited by Lisa Hiley and Deborah Burns
Cover design by Alethea Morrison
Art direction and text design by Cynthia N. McFarland
Text production by Cynthia N. McFarland and Jennifer Jepson Smith

Illustrations by Jo Anna Rissanen
Arena diagrams by Ilona Sherratt
Indexed by Nancy D. Wood

Be sure to read all instructions thoroughly before attempting any of the activities in this book, especially if you are inexperienced in handling horses. No book can replace the guidance of an expert horseman nor can it anticipate every situation that will arise. Always be cautious and vigilant when working with a large and unpredictable animal.

Storey Publishing
210 MASS MoCA Way
North Adams, MA 01247
www.storey.com

Printed in the United States by Versa Press
10 9 8 7 6 5

LIBRARY OF CONGRESS CATALOGING-IN-PUBLICATION DATA

Ballou, Jec Aristotle.
   Equine fitness / Jec Aristotle Ballou.
      p. cm.
   Includes bibliographical references and index.
   ISBN 978-1-60342-463-9 (pbk. : alk. paper)
   1. Horses—Health. 2. Horses—Exercise. I. Title.
SF285.3.B35 2010
636.1'0893—dc22
                              2009023864

Dedication & Acknowledgments

My most heartfelt gratitude goes to the numerous horses along the way that have taught me new ways to see things or given a little extra in their effort. It's these kinds of horses that make a trainer always want to increase the scope of her abilities. Through them, I have been able to keep raising the bar on equine athletic performance and I am thankful for this. Specifically, thanks to Catamac's Cat, a mare to whom my debt will never be repaid!

My second nod of gratitude goes to my teachers both here and abroad. Their patience and perseverance in the selfless act of teaching have often fueled my enthusiasm to continue working with horses and riders. I especially thank Manolo Mendez for always advocating the horse's best interests. Thanks also to Dr. Sherry Ackerman, W. Charles Ballou, and the community of exceptional horsemen and horsewomen I grew up with at the Green Mountain Horse Association in Woodstock, Vermont. Many have gone on to represent the United States in international competitions; I am in awe of their humble roots.

Lastly, I would like to acknowledge my colleagues and clients who work tirelessly on the horse's behalf. Thanks to Mark Schuerman, Naomi Johnston, Rachel Anicetti, David Lichman, Home At Last Sanctuary, Katherine Curran, and Storey Publishing.

CONTENTS

INTRODUCTION 1

1. How the Muscles Work 5

2. General Rules of Fitness 16

3. Schooling vs. Conditioning 31
   CONDITIONING EXERCISES 37
   1. Spiraling In and Out
   2. Sprint Lines
   3. Strengthening the Front End
   4. Legging Up
   5. Transitioning Downward
   6. Temporomandibular Joint (TMJ) Massage
   7. Loops and Poles (David Lichman)
   8. Waltzing with Your Horse (Sherry Ackerman)
   9. Gearing Up to Gallop (Yvonne Barteau)

4. Posture Determines Strength 47
   STRENGTHENING EXERCISES 55
   10. Rein-Back up a Hill
   11. Rein-Back on a Curve
   12. Turn on the Forehand in Motion
   13. Exercise on a Slope
   14. Riding a Drop
   15. Canter to Walk Downhill (Gina Miles)
   16. Gymnastic Jumping
   17. Sets and Reps for Arena (Jennifer Bryant)
   18. Double Longe (Mark Schuerman)
   19. Arena Interval Training

5. Warming Up and Cooling Down 69
   WARM-UP EXERCISES 73
   20. Tail Pull
   21. Tail Rotations
   22. Lateral Cervical Flexion (Jim Masterson)
   23. Shoulder Release Down and Back (Jim Masterson)
   24. Shoulder Release Down and Forward (Jim Masterson)
   25. Loosening the Back
   26. Warm-up 1 — The Oval
   27. Warm-up 2 — Simple Trot Pattern
   28. Shoulder-In to Shallow Serpentine (Betsy Steiner)
   29. Canter on the Honor System (Jessica Jahiel)

6. The Mighty Neck 87

NECK EXERCISES 93

    30. Horizontal Frame Conditioning

    31. Changing Speeds

    32. Counter Canter Loops

    33. Counter Canter Serpentines

    34. Shoulder-In Repetitions

    35. Shoulder-In Traveling Out (Manolo Mendez)

    36. Striding In, Striding Out

7. The Stifle Is Critical 102

STIFLE EXERCISES 107

    37. Trotting Poles in an Arc

    38. Pick-up Sticks

    39. Lifting the Hind Legs

    40. Bringing the Hind Legs Forward

    41. Stepping Over Slowly

    42. Cantering on Uneven Terrain

    43. In and Out Leg-Yielding (Becky Hart)

8. Time to Stretch 115

STRETCHING EXERCISES 117

    44. Shoulder Rotation Stretch

    45. Rear-Leg Circles

    46. Pelvis Tucks

    47. Poll Stretch

    48. Hip Stretch

    49. Shoulder Circles

    50. Bladder Meridian Exercise for Tension Release (Jim Masterson)

EXERCISE ROUTINES 126

FOUR FITNESS GOALS 128

GLOSSARY 130

CONTRIBUTOR BIOGRAPHIES 132

RESOURCES 133

INDEX 134

PULLOUT EXERCISE CARDS . . . . following page 136

INTRODUCTION

My interest in properly conditioning horses for their respective disciplines has developed over the years not only from riding and loving these animals but also from being an athlete myself. When you commit yourself, your horse, or both to a training plan, you soon realize how many unexpected bumps there are in the road. Even the best-laid plans can unravel. You may find yourself hitting a plateau in training, wondering why you are not advancing or why your horse seems sore or sour. This book will help you assess your progress and find the answers to many training questions and problems.

Having won championships in basketball, rowing, and mountain biking, as well as several equestrian disciplines, I have come to appreciate the straightforward but painstaking effort that goes into preparing an athlete to perform at his or her highest level. It matters not whether the event in question is a local fund-raiser or an international competition. What matters is that the athlete can perform in peak condition, with a happy attitude, and recover well, which means no prolonged period of soreness.

In my lifetime with horses, I have observed that the equine industry has become compartmental-

ized, with trainers and horses focusing exclusively on single disciplines. Daily workouts primarily address exercises or maneuvers specific to that discipline, to the detriment of focused and sustained time spent on overall equine fitness requirements. This situation is similar to a human gymnast practicing handsprings and splits repetitiously, day after day, but losing sight of the larger picture that he needs to consider, which is his ongoing *basic fitness*, beyond the particular demands of his chosen sport.

When overly specific training techniques are used with horses, the rider or trainer may determine that the horse is not making progress and diagnose the problem as a schooling shortfall. Much of the time, however, the issue is not necessarily one of inadequate schooling; it is more a matter of insufficient basic fitness, whether the problem is strength, coordination, or suppleness.

Maintaining your horse's physical structure and cardiovascular aptitude (including stamina, recovery, and adaptability to stress) to the best of your ability will keep him happily and comfortably performing his job at the highest level. This is just as (if not more) important as undertaking an adequate amount of specialized training to meet the requirements of your chosen discipline. In many cases, addressing your horse's underlying fitness can resolve many of the frustrating stumbling blocks that crop up along the way during any well-laid training plan. Be aware that even with the best schooling and conditioning plans, other factors such as boarding conditions and nutrition also affect your horse's health and fitness.

Structuring Your Horse's Daily Life

Most of us do not have the luxury of keeping our horses on our own property, which necessitates boarding them at commercial facilities. Any boarding situation comes with pluses and minuses. The main point to keep in mind when choosing a boarding facility is that your horse's daily living conditions impact his overall well-being as much as the most well-intentioned training and conditioning plan.

Many owners make decisions about boarding based on budget or convenience. Within those constraints, I always emphasize to my students that it is crucial to put the horse's needs above all else when choosing where to house him. In the end, this will make your life with him much easier. For instance, a horse who eats insufficient hay, lives in a cramped stall, and is surrounded by a stressful environment will go only so far in his career, even with the world's best training. Daily handling, a regular feeding routine, access to turnout, and the opportunity to socialize are part of the equation that keeps a horse mentally and physically prepared for his job. They are *equally* as important as his time working in the arena.

In California, where I live and train, very few boarding facilities have areas for turnout, which means many horses have to stand around in box stalls most of the time. A horse that is forced to live almost entirely in a resting state suffers from a decrease in circulation of blood, oxygen, joint fluid, and so on, which stresses his body and digestive tract, just as with humans who lead sedentary lives. This physical discomfort begins to affect the horse mentally. He becomes agitated, full of pent-up energy, or bored. He may become hard to handle or develop vices such as pawing, kicking at walls, or chewing wood.

Negative emotional states put more stress on the body and limit how much the horse is able to gain from his workouts. A stressed, hyperactive horse cannot relax and use his muscles in the way this book encourages. This is why the horse's living environment must be factored into the entire training and conditioning equation.

KEEP THEM MOVING

My own solution to easing the effects of box-stall living is to keep the horses I have in training moving around as much as possible during the day, and to make sure they receive the most natural, sugar-free diet available. In addition to their workouts, they are hand walked each afternoon regardless of the weather, and I sometimes tie them outside in the sun to graze. If I am teaching a lesson, I may walk around with or sit on a horse that would otherwise just be in his stall. The stalls at my barn are oriented so that horses can see each other, touch noses, and socialize all day.

A healthy horse is a happy horse. And a happy horse is one that wants to perform for you. This has been proven to me repeatedly through the years, so I urge you to make your horse's life mirror as closely as possible what it would be like in the wild — forage diet, lots of movement, socialization, and consistent handling. You will surely see a difference in your horse's overall attitude and general health.

A Few Words about Nutrition

What you put in your horse directly affects what he can put out in terms of performance. Feeding the right amount of good-quality food is a critical link in the fitness equation. I am not going to give my personal advice for *what* to feed your horse; a huge number of books and articles on the topic already exist.

Furthermore, there is a lot of controversy surrounding nutrition, including arguments against carbohydrates, colliding opinions about alfalfa, discussions about how much to supplement your horse, debates about the limitations of supplements, and so on. Although I am not going to add my voice to the various opinions swirling around, I would like to provide a few indisputable guidelines for feeding your horse.

Keep the following information in mind not only at home but when choosing a boarding facility. A facility's feeding practices will impact your horse's performance, mental attitude, and how much you're able to enjoy him. It's important that you speak up about what you want and need for your horse.

Avoid Concentrated Feeds

The equine digestive system can't handle over-processed foods with sweeteners and fillers like dried corn. These substances tax your horse's system and provide almost no nourishment to his body for exercise. Look for grain products with only a few ingredients and no major sweeteners, such as hulled oats, flax, timothy pellets, and so on.

Feed Hay, Hay, and More Hay

Your horse's entire diet should be forage based (hay or grass). Grain, pellets, or supplements should be used in small amounts to make up for deficiencies in the protein or mineral content of your hay.

Check Hay Content Regularly

There are many labs that do this for a small fee. The sugar and protein content of hay changes drastically throughout a harvest season and in different weather patterns. Have it checked every four months so that you know *what* you are feeding.

Be Realistic about Intake

When a horse reduces his activity level, whether through injury or because his rider is too busy, adjust his caloric intake. Do not keep feeding him the same amount as when he is active.

Feed Frequently

Horses are meant to graze up to 17 hours per day. Their stomachs become very acidic when they have to endure long stretches of time between feedings, as is commonly the case in modern stabling arrangements. Feed forage at least three times per day to keep the stomach less acidic, which will help keep ulcers, agitated behavior, and irregular energy at bay.

Moisten Food

Add water to the grain/supplements you feed your horse, making a mash. This assists in neutralizing stomach acidity, makes feed more easily digestible, and helps hydrate your horse.

Add Salt and Minerals

Horses in rigorous exercise programs need to replenish electrolytes lost during the day. But don't go overboard with lots of commercial pastes and powders. The best solution is a good trace mineral added to their feed.

Pure Celtic Sea Salt (available in health food stores) is a moist and highly digestible form of salt that provides over 80 vital trace minerals. One to three teaspoons added to your horse's feed each day will balance and replenish electrolyte levels and also encourage your horse to drink water.

Watch the Treats!

Many commercial horse cookies are overly processed and too sugary. While seemingly small, just a few handfuls of these treats can spike a horse's blood-sugar levels and affect digestion. Stick with natural goodies such as apples, but, even then, don't overdo it.

Keep Youngsters Lean

Don't make the mistake of overfeeding young horses in an effort to get them to "grow" or "fill out." One- and two-year-olds are best kept lean and gawky looking so that their joints do not have to bear too much weight as they're forming. This way, their joints develop and close properly.

All for One and One for All

Let's put aside our respective hats — be they cowboy hats, hunter caps, or dressage derbies — and look at the horse for what he is: an impressive athlete of mighty muscle and bone. And while we're at it, let's recognize that he functions best when all his parts operate smoothly to benefit the whole. His body is an interconnected unit. It functions as a whole and must be trained as a whole. The efficiency of one part depends on the strength and suppleness of neighboring parts.

This book aims to give readers general guidelines for improving their horse's natural movement and thereby creating better equine athletes. I call this optimal way of going "healthy movement" because it is the healthiest way for the horse to perform and, therefore, paramount to his overall well-being. Fancy or exaggerated movement for the sake of showing a horse or winning a competition must never be favored over making the horse a stronger, more fit, and better-balanced athlete overall.

CREATE YOUR OWN ROUTINE

After you've read this book, you'll be able to use the exercises contained within it to develop your own fitness and conditioning routines based on the needs of your own horse(s). At the back of the book, you'll find nearly all of the exercises on perforated pullout pages, one exercise per card. You can follow my recommendations on pages 126–27 or create your own exercise program that can change as your horse progresses.

CHAPTER 1

HOW THE MUSCLES WORK

I T FREQUENTLY SURPRISES ME how little most equestrians seem to know about how their horses' muscular systems function. Too few riders seem able to distinguish the croup from the trapezius or the serratus from the quadriceps. Many riding frustrations can be avoided and questions can be answered with a rudimentary understanding of basic anatomy and muscle function, so it is important to understand how and why the horse's body does or does not respond to what we ask of it every day. You cannot rely on what you see from the outside.

Horses can continue physical activity even in the presence of muscle/body tightness and mild discomfort. In fact, to some observers, they will appear 100 percent fit. In the presence of tightness, however, as we humans know, other ailments are just around the corner. Muscle tightness leads to an entire chain reaction as the body tries to adapt. Tightness in the lower back, for example, will soon evolve from localized discomfort into a notable change in a person's stride and posture.

That change in posture will create tightness elsewhere in the body, such as the hamstrings or the base of the neck. As these areas of tension spread, the overall mechanism quickly loses its optimal functioning ability and its aptitude for top performance is hindered.

Think of the equine muscles as big elastic bands. Although a horse may appear to be moving just fine based on the outward observation of his gaits, the real story is often that those elastic bands are compromised in some way — brittle, stiff, about to break, etc. Because horses cannot speak, we must always put a great deal of thought into whether our daily activities are likely to create tightness in a specific muscle group that will rapidly translate into decreased performance and discomfort.

Just because we cannot *see* the tightness does not mean it isn't there! The muscle group could be malfunctioning. Any muscle that is not entirely toned, loose, and in harmony with its surrounding muscle groups is *working against the horse*.

Muscles Don't Act Alone

When we talk about a horse "using" his body, we need to keep in mind the interdependence of the horse's bones, tendons, ligaments, and muscles. Although we often talk about the strength or engagement of certain muscles for certain exercises, the muscles are only one part of the equation. Because muscles attach to the horse's bones, they are responsible for producing all skeletal movement. In addition, muscles are arranged in pairs.

Suppose one muscle in a muscle pair contracts momentarily to move the bone of the horse's foreleg. For this muscle's function to be correct and smooth, it must immediately relax the contraction entirely so that its corresponding muscle can contract and pull the bone back in the opposite direction. The first muscle must be completely relaxed and stretchy so that it provides no opposition to the second muscle as it contracts. All skeletal motion must flow in this way. You can understand where existing tightness would block this flow!

Muscles also extend into tendons, which are responsible for controlling and moving the joints. This interplay between muscles and tendons is critical. For a horse not to break down or sustain a major injury, his tendons must remain elastic and pliable. Otherwise, tendon or joint strain will result. Tendons themselves, however, do not possess much elasticity. The necessary elasticity to safeguard them and their corresponding joints comes from the muscles associated with them.

When a horse operates with tight muscles, his muscle fibers are shorter and more contracted than they should be; therefore, they cannot stretch as readily or quickly as they need to. This tightening then spreads from one muscle group to another because as one group tightens, the neigh-

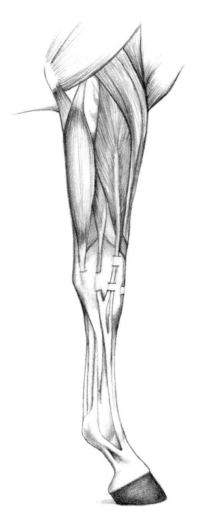

Tight muscles can and will pass along tightness or failure to neighboring muscle groups.

A tight shoulder muscle is most often to blame for a strained tendon in the lower leg.

boring muscle group is not able to stretch enough to accommodate the necessary movement. This second group will then tighten and will pass along the stress to the next muscle group, and so on, creating a ripple effect.

For example, during a horse's basic exercise and movement, tight shoulder muscles will pass along this tightness to the upper arm muscles and eventually down to the digital flexors and tendons. Inevitably, the horse will suffer a tendon strain or tear. And while the temptation will probably be to blame footing or a freak accident for the strain, the truth is more likely to be that the horse's tight shoulder muscles were the original source of the breakdown. Their tightness spread to neighboring muscles and then down into the supporting tendons, the smaller, more fragile structures that soon broke down. In an opposite scenario, when a properly conditioned horse slips or missteps, he is far less likely to suffer an injury because his muscles are more toned and, therefore, elastic, allowing more "give" in the soft tissue at the moment of trauma.

Don't Blame the Last Thing You Did

In the case of injuries or fatigue, horse owners commonly look at the animal's most recent activities to gauge why a body part either broke down or isn't working at 100 percent. This is not always, or even very often, an accurate indicator. Especially where muscles and exercise are involved, an animal's most recent activity is unlikely to be the cause of a current failing, although a minor incident might have initiated it.

Muscle strains or spasms frequently start out very tiny. They can begin as just a few contracted fibers within a muscle, arising from a slip in the paddock or trailer to pulling back on the crossties or resistance under saddle. In fact, numerous motions that might occur outside of training or competition can cause tightening or contraction, which is then aggravated by further exercise. This aggravation is cumulative. Although the horse will continue to move and perform adequately,

that tiny spasm will keep recruiting more fibers, even though to the naked eye the horse will seem just fine. Because it is cumulative, the spasm or strain will keep building over time.

The intensity of the horse's working conditions determines how long it will be until this increasing discomfort begins to affect his gait, performance, and attitude. Sometimes, it could take a month or more for a spasm or strain to noticeably manifest itself. This is why it is critical to thoroughly know the conditions under which your horse lives, works, and plays. You can then begin to trace back any minor discomfort to its probable source, recalling that it is most likely not the most recent activity.

KEY POINT Physical discomfort not only detracts from the horse's performance and quality of movement, it also greatly affects his attitude and temperament. A horse that does not feel 100 percent functional and harmonious in his body will often become ill-tempered about his work and what is being asked of him. This is the most frequent cause of behaviors such as balking, bucking, and refusing. If it doesn't feel good, he won't want to do it!

Understanding Muscle Structure

To understand how muscles function, it's helpful to have a basic picture of them in mind to remind us that they are not like the cogs of a machine that just keep working, working, working. In fact, they are elaborate and somewhat delicate structures.

Every muscle has two ends and a belly. Generally, when most people think of muscles, they picture only the belly — the biggest, bulkiest part; however, the two tapered ends of a muscle are just as, if not more, important in muscle function and helping it become stronger. One of these ends attaches to a bone and is called the "origin" of the muscle. It is the anchor for the muscle's movement. The other end, the "insertion," is more flexible and inserts into other tissues (i.e., tendons,

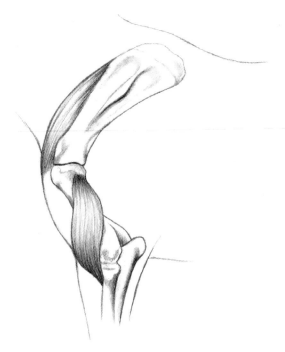

Muscles are stressed most at their tapered ends where they attach to bone or tendon.

other muscles). This is where the motion takes place that is created by the power action of the muscle's belly.

The most common point for stress within a muscle is at the origin end. As a muscle nears the bone to which it anchors, it merges with tendons at the attachment point. Given the less-elastic nature of tendons compared with muscle fibers, these areas are more adversely affected by stress and are generally the first to suffer from strenuous activity.

Meanwhile, the belly of the muscle often fares fine. As muscles tighten or shorten from regular exercise, however, the amount of stress placed on these already-stressed anchor areas increases. Over time, this cumulative stress will adversely affect the joint, eventually producing joint pain and, finally, visible signs of discomfort in the horse's overall way of moving and performing.

The success of any conditioning program comes from the horse's body adapting progressively to the stress load of a chosen exercise. If a horse performs the same amount and type of exercise every day, he will maintain a certain level of fitness but will not improve on that level. To increase his level of fitness, a horse must undergo strategic increases in his workouts and then be allowed to adapt to the increase before he is asked for further changes. In this way, his adaptive response to greater exercise happens progressively.

Generally, horses should not perform the same type of conditioning exercises on consecutive days. This will allow for repair of minor tissue damage from a given workout before again putting the same structures under stress.

Muscles and Oxygen Intake

Paramount in all conditioning work, but particularly in strengthening the muscles, is the deep and regular intake of oxygen. This is a simple, yet often overlooked, aspect of equine exercise. Just like humans, horses are occasionally prone to breathing in a shallow manner or even holding their breath. Incomplete and inefficient breathing hinders the body's ability to build healthy muscle and become stronger.

Also just like a human athlete, the horse cannot relax and oxygenate his muscles without breathing deeply. Therefore, he will never fully develop his body, and he will hit a training or conditioning plateau because he will be working with a tight or restricted body. Unfortunately, this pattern of short or shallow breathing can quickly become a habit.

When a horse breathes shallowly, his stride is stiff, his chest pushes out, and his hind legs trail far behind his body mass. Schooling him like this will only make him stiffer rather than strengthening him. Until the horse breathes properly, his musculature will not fill out adequately and his gaits will appear stilted instead of fluid. The cure is to supply the body with proper oxygen! Sometimes, this means giving him frequent walk breaks, riding him in a different tempo, or avoiding work that brings him tension.

You can encourage better breathing and athletic development by being more methodical in your training sessions. Above all, learn to take note of your horse's breathing, asking the following questions:

✓ How many minutes into each session does it take for your horse to blow through his nose?

✓ How frequently does he do this when you are riding?

✓ When you halt him and let out the reins, does he sigh?

✓ Does he sigh when you're in motion?

✓ At the trot, can you feel his rib cage expanding and deflating under your legs?

When handling your horse on the ground, make a note of his breathing patterns. Is he relaxed and breathing through his nose on the cross-ties before you ride? Can you see his rib cage moving deeply in and out or does he appear to be holding his jaw and lips tightly and have his body in a defensive posture? When you longe your horse, does he hold his breath? Some horses will hold their breath during early stages of the canter, evidenced by a grunt or heaving noise at every stride. If this is the case, you will want to execute several transitions into and out of the canter followed by walk rests until he begins, with time, to blow through his nose and relax his rib cage.

Especially in early work, a young horse develops habits in how he approaches his work, either breathing in a deep and relaxed manner or holding his breath. This is why it is critical to ensure that the initial training in a horse's career, in addition to using proper-fitting equipment, establishes a foundation of relaxation along with performance so that he does not form long-standing habits that inhibit respiration and thereby strength building. This step should be as much a part of your young horse's foundation training as other routine activities such as learning ground manners and sacking out.

With older horses who have had harsh or inconsistent training and exhibit tension in their breathing, you will need to go back to basics for a period of time. Your best bet is to create a very reliable day-to-day routine (for example, 10 minutes of longeing followed by 25 minutes of riding in all three gaits with very basic exercises). As your horse begins to understand the reliable — and repetitive — expectations for his daily workout, you should be able to see his breathing change for the better.

KEY POINT Once you begin to pay attention to your horse's breathing patterns, it will become second nature to you. Do not move on from an exercise on any given day until his breathing is full, deep, and relaxed. By doing so, you will teach him to keep himself properly oxygenated at all times, with the added benefit that he will be less mentally stressed.

How Muscles Grow Stronger

A muscle never *adds* fibers to its composition but rather becomes stronger by enlarging the fibers it already has. As these fibers enlarge, they also increase their metabolic processes such as utilizing fuels for energy, more efficient cooling and recovery, and flushing out waste products from the soft tissue and blood. This enlargement of fibers increases both the motive power of a muscle and the absorption of the nutrition necessary to maintain that power.

To reach this point, it is necessary that a muscle regularly be used at 75 percent of maximum tension for a prolonged period. Easy exercise, even every day, does not build muscle. Conversely, prolonged or excessive tension only fatigues a muscle and does nothing to enlarge its fibers. When too much tension is present, metabolic substances fail to nourish muscle fibers as necessary and, rather than becoming stronger, muscle fibers will shrink over time. Waste products will accumulate in the tissue, which cannot handle the added load.

As this happens, the alternating contraction–relaxation process for each muscle diminishes. Spasms in these tight muscles interfere with the flow of oxygen and reduce the capacity of the muscles to flush out toxins and waste products, which in turn affects performance in both the fit and unfit horse.

In an unfit horse, working with too much tension will result in early fatigue, or "fading," during a riding session. In the more fit horse, in contrast, muscles begin to tighten up and he loses coordination and power. Muscle function begins to deteriorate, both immediately and for the long term. Following an incorrect workout, the muscles will begin to spasm as the horse cools out and blood is drawn away from them. These spasms do not go away by themselves. They continue and may increase in size and/or intensity until revised exercise or massage relieves the built-up stress.

Achieving Fitness

As stated above, light or easy exercise, even on an ongoing schedule, will never increase your horse's strength or fitness. It *is*, however, good for his circulation, mental well-being, and, sometimes, weight loss. When actual fitness is called for, you need to put the horse's muscular system under the right amount of stress — enough to put his muscle fibers under 75 percent of maximum tension, but not more than that and not for an excessive period of time. After each workout session, you need to allow enough time to flush out waste products to prevent deterioration of metabolic processes and shrinking/weakening of fibers as outlined above. The length and intensity of a training session and

Exercising a horse with too much tension does not increase strength. This horse is being pushed to the point of tension, which compromises his entire posture. His hind legs trail behind, indicating that his topline muscles are not working properly.

the time needed for recovery vary according to the horse's age, health, and current level of fitness and will change over time as those factors change.

Measurably increasing a horse's fitness level and strength requires sustained effort over a period of months, not days or weeks. An animal's soft tissue requires this time frame to adapt to structural and metabolic changes and, therefore, mandates a period of consistent conditioning. Bear in mind, however, that *tension does not equal strength*. Many well-intentioned riders exercise their horses with too hurried a tempo, on demanding footing, in a stressful environment, or under other conditions that force the horse into a state of tension, either in a particular muscle group or overall.

Naively assuming that any amount of exercise is better than none and therefore will make him stronger/fitter, a rider may fail to note whether her horse's muscular system is conducting itself with *tone* as opposed to *tension*. Remember, too much tension will do no more good for fitness than letting your horse stand in the pasture! In addition, tension does not mean that a horse is using his muscles correctly. In fact, it indicates the opposite.

KEY POINT All conditioning programs build on a horse's genetic material; they do not add to it. You cannot make a sprinter out of a horse with slow-twitch muscles or an endurance athlete out of one with an inefficient metabolic system.

This horse is working with proper tone and no tension, as shown by his rounded topline, reaching neck, and extended legs. His muscles are able to receive blood and oxygen and efficiently flush out metabolic waste, thereby becoming stronger.

As muscles work during exercise, they warm up and eventually begin to produce excess heat that is released in the form of perspiration. As sweat accumulates it moves the hair directly overlaying a particular muscle, which accounts for the "crushed velvet" or swirly appearance of a horse's coat after vigorous exercise.

Observing the placement of these sweaty areas — or chronic sweat patterns — can provide some useful information. If you notice that your horse sweats in some areas of his body but not in others, this tells you which muscles he is using during your workouts and whether he is engaging the correct ones to become stronger.

Ideally, the horse should show sweat in his "ring of muscles," meaning his back, neck, croup, and abdomen. This nearly circular muscle and ligament system controls, among other aspects of balance and athletic ability, the horse's locomotion. (See chapter 4 for more on the ring of muscles.) As he becomes stronger, his post-workout sweat marks should move from the lower areas of his hindquar-ters to higher up around his hips and croup to demonstrate that he is using and developing his larger, more powerful locomotive areas. This means that the horse's flank/hip area should be quite sweaty as opposed to just his gaskin and stifle area.

I have heard many skeptics over the years try to debunk the theory of sweat patterns, asserting that some breeds in particular just have certain whorls in their hair when they work out and that it has nothing to do with how they use their bodies. If you are among these doubters, let me say that this theory of sweat patterns is nothing new. If you read classical literature about training horses, you will find mention of it. More importantly, I have never worked with a horse whose sweat patterns didn't change when he started to use his body differently.

Try it for yourself. Exercise your horse for one month in a different (hopefully, correct!) posture/frame every day for 30 minutes or more and you will indisputably notice changes in both *where* he sweats and *how* he sweats.

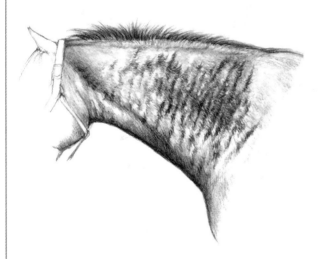 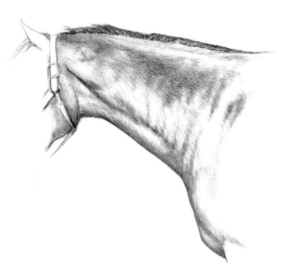

The horse on the left has a ruffled sweat pattern and the hairs don't follow the direction of normal neck muscling. The horse on the right shows the same degree of sweatiness, but the hairs lie smoothly in the direction of the muscles.

What does this mean? The first horse was most likely braced or crooked in his neck during his workout, causing his asymmetrical sweat pattern. The second horse was using his neck muscles evenly and in harmony with their natural structures.

I see this often with riders demanding that their horses be "on the bit" or carry their bodies in a tight frame even though overall fitness is lacking. Although the horse does pull his neck into a rounded outline, it happens through tension — not alignment and balance as it should. The rest of his body is not fit enough to support the posture. As the top neck muscles become tense to hold the posture, the bottom neck muscles brace and pull upward (rather than remaining passive as they should in a preferable scenario). With these two muscle groups essentially opposing each other, respiration and blood flow are restricted; consequently, the horse's neck vertebrae become stiff. Continuing to ride in this manner weakens the entire spine and impairs the horse's ability to move well.

KEY POINT Strain does not equal gain! Just because your horse's muscles are tense when you ride does not mean they are getting stronger, and brief bursts of rigorous activity that create a lot of sweat do not guarantee an appreciable gain in strength.

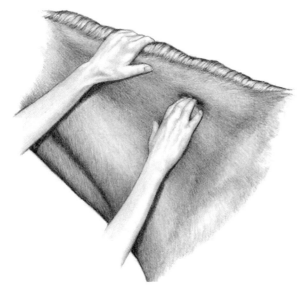

Muscles should not be rock hard to the touch. They should feel firm but pliable.

Making the Right Demands

By overly tensing certain areas of their bodies, horses have an uncanny ability to satisfy our demands when we ride them. We must, therefore, be sure our demands are the right ones! Just like humans, equine athletes can conduct themselves with compromised muscle groups, shallow breathing, and an unrelaxed mind throughout exercises and workouts. And rather than becoming more fit or stronger day to day, they become more compromised in the body, more stiff, and, if anything, less fit. This is why, as riders, we must ascertain the difference between putting the horse's body under strain and tension and working it in a relaxed gymnastic manner.

For example, most arena and trail riders prefer their horses to have a "big" trot that feels powerful and covers ground; however, if a rider tries to achieve such a trot with her horse before he has adequate balance and symmetry on both sides of his body, the horse will compromise himself in meeting these demands. As his front legs take increasingly longer strides, his hindquarters, lacking sufficient strength and suppleness at this time, will fall out of sync. His hind legs will begin to trail out behind his body and his pelvis will tilt backwards, straining the lower back. Then, not only will the horse bear undue weight on the front legs, he will most often push his body more toward one diagonal than the other and use his body asymmetrically to compensate for weakness and balance on one side. With so much force on his forehand, his shoulder muscles will tighten, setting him up for injuries. The result: deteriorated overall movement.

Admittedly, brief moments of tension are to be expected when teaching the equine athlete new material or pushing his body to limits beyond his ordinary routine; however, the rider/trainer must ensure that these moments are only *brief*. A tight or restricted body, kept in that state too long, will detract from performance. When a horse is not allowed to physically develop slowly, his body will compromise to meet the demand. Over time, he will become sore and break down. Remember that building strength takes time!

The Difference between "Good" Muscle and "Bad" Muscle

As your horse's fitness improves, it becomes important to ask *how* it's improving. Muscles can enlarge in a way that does not produce healthy shape or tone. Learn to make note of whether your horse's muscles feel like rocks or they possess healthy tone without being too hard. Good aerobic muscle should be firm to the touch but still pliable. It should not feel like rock. Muscles that feel hard are starved of oxygen and evidence that the horse has been worked too much in tension. They have built up shape by bracing rather than by the engagement/release sequence described earlier. These are sometimes referred to as "dry" muscles because of their lack of pliability.

The bulk and hardness of the tissue is not an indicator of strength. Rock-hard muscles are not only at more risk for tear and injury, they are not able to stretch well or flush out waste buildup. By overworking certain areas of his body, a

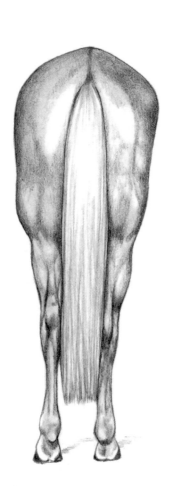

This horse's left hip and flank show more muscling than the right.

Here the right side is over-developed, with the right shoulder larger than the left.

Viewed from above, the asymmetry of the left side is apparent.

horse will sometimes develop healthy muscles in some areas while developing overly hard and depleted muscles elsewhere. This means that there is not smooth functioning among muscle groups. This unevenness is another good reason to keep a continuous inventory of your horse's fitness developments.

An analogy can be drawn here to human athletes. Those with muscles that appear to be bulging are not generally the strongest or most fit. Think of the nimble triathlete, the supple ballerina, or the lean 100-mile cyclist. With their smooth, correctly aerobic muscling, these athletes are not only very strong, but their bodies are well oxygenated and their muscles stretchy. They are the embodiment of athleticism.

"Good" muscling is not too bulky and, when pressed under your fingertip, should feel like a firm pillow. It should be resilient and "give" under your touch, although it should not feel spongy or shapeless like a fat deposit. It should feel toned yet moveable, as if you could almost pluck it or move it around with your finger, rather than feeling as though it is stuck by concrete to your horse's skeleton.

The Importance of Symmetry

In my years of training horses, I have yet to come across one that is completely symmetrical, meaning that he uses both sides of his body evenly. As with humans, horses are generally one-sided and slightly crooked. Some are obviously more so than others. Opinions vary about the reasons for this inherent one-sidedness.

Some trainers, for instance, believe lifelong crookedness can be traced back to how unborn foals lie in the womb. Others believe that we humans make them crooked by repeatedly leading and mounting from their left sides. The actual reasons for their asymmetry don't really matter. What does matter is that riders pay attention to it and do everything in their power to assist their horses in using both sides of their bodies evenly.

Most horses will quickly show you their asymmetry by strongly preferring to travel in a particular direction. If this is not addressed swiftly, the horse will develop muscling that is asymmetrical to match the crookedness in his body. For example, the muscling on the left side of his neck and along his flank will be contracted and shorter than the muscling on his right side. Alternatively, what frequently happens is that a horse simply develops *more* muscling on one side of his body. This comes about by performing his exercises in a one-sided manner.

Obviously, when the muscling is uneven, it pulls the horse's skeleton slightly out of balance and the horse is then no longer able to move in a decent posture. These imbalances might go undetected to a novice horse person without a keen eye.

When a horse presents crookedness and correlating asymmetrical muscling, a rider must work to get him to *relax* the dominant side of his body while engaging more on the weaker side. This does *not* mean exercising him more in his weaker direction, which only leads to greater fatigue and imbalance on that side. Instead, stretching is most often the answer. One-sidedness means that a horse's musculature is longer on one side of his body and shorter on the other side. The side he leans toward is his longer side (for example: if your horse always bends his neck to the right and leans toward the left, his left side is the longer side and the right is shorter).

To remedy the problem, you want to stretch his shorter side more than the longer one. When a horse tends to overuse one side of his body, the opposite/weaker side is generally blocked or stiffer, which prevents it from being as engaged and functional as the dominant side. Strategic stretching, both mounted and on the ground, will go far in alleviating asymmetry. When unclear about what type of stretching to use, garner the help of an equine massage therapist or trainer. (See chapter 8 for more on massage.)

2

GENERAL RULES OF FITNESS

Bringing a horse to an adequate level of fitness for everyday riding takes more effort and planning than many riders realize. Perhaps because horses cannot talk to us or because they seem like large masses of bone and muscle, we tend to regard them as being naturally more apt for their job than they actually are. We jump into specializations with them and neglect good basic conditioning, which puts them at a disadvantage. Too frequently, riders treat their horses like cars — turn on the engine and go. This chapter provides conditioning tips and information that is sometimes overlooked in our own busy lives and dealings with horses.

It is easy to look at a horse of average weight that shows some muscling and assume that he is plenty fit for whatever you may ask in your daily riding; however, we far too often underestimate what does or does not physically tax horses. You must see past the initial impressions of a big, powerful-looking horse. Size and brawn don't much matter when it comes to the aptitude of tendons, bones, and ligaments for the job at hand, no matter the job. In other words, it's impossible to judge a horse's physical preparedness by what you think you see on the outside.

Because of the fragility of their vertebral columns, many horses require several months of exercise for their back and abdominal muscles to gain the necessary strength to maintain a good posture under the rider's weight. If the muscles of his back and abdomen are not developed properly, the horse bears a rider's weight by overtensing the tendinous floor of his belly like a sling, creating a dropped back and saggy underline, which is very difficult to change. Furthermore, it can take up to *a year* to develop the fitness necessary to handle an hour's worth of walk, trot, and canter. Yet, how many riders require this after just a few months?

KEY POINT If you don't pay careful attention to your horse's daily aptitude and physical needs, you are forsaking the needs inherent in his athletic development. As stewards of these fine animals, we owe it to them to keep this information foremost in our dealings with them, no matter how large and powerful they may appear.

Assessing Fitness

When a horse undergoes time off because of weather, injury, or rider time constraints, he loses fitness fast. Before bringing him back into regular exercise, it is necessary to determine where he stands in his fitness level. To develop an appropriate training and workout schedule, it is helpful to ascertain whether the horse is very unfit, somewhat out of shape, or moderately fit. Assessing a baseline of fitness is also necessary when you buy a new horse, start riding a friend's, or have never really thought about your horse's overall fitness before. Use the following steps to assess overall fitness.

Check Attitude and Behavior

Generally speaking, horses are among the kindest animals in the animal kingdom. When resistances arise during training, the majority of the time the cause is a physical ailment of one kind or another. In spite of our fondness for anthropomorphizing horses (attributing human feelings and behaviors to them), horses have no cognition for acting naughty. When they do so, it is often out of physical discomfort.

In particular, when a horse suddenly begins to exhibit a bad behavior after having been in training for a period, the reason is most likely discomfort either from soreness, fatigue, or pain that may be arising from saddle fit, strain, or undetected injury. Regardless of the cause, his movement will always suffer and a rider must be laser sharp to recognize when he is not performing at his optimal level. A small ailment can rapidly turn into a major one that sidelines a horse if not addressed promptly.

Determine Cardio Fitness

A heart-rate monitor is an immensely useful tool here, although a stethoscope works perfectly well (see box on page 19). Take the horse's heart rate immediately following a round of moderately strenuous exercise, such as trotting actively in the arena for 15 minutes straight followed by a lap of canter in each direction, or a 3-mile (5 km) trail ride doing at least a trot pace. His heart rate should be about 120 to 140.

Let him stand or walk slowly for 5 minutes and take the heart rate again. In a reasonably fit horse, the heart rate will be around 60 beats per minute after a few minutes of recovery. If your horse's heart rate is still above 72 beats per minute after the 5-minute rest period, it most likely indicates that the work was beyond your horse's current level of conditioning.

Determine Rate of Perceived Exertion

You can use a series of exercises from this book to evaluate whether the horse feels that the task requires:

1. No effort
2. Slight effort
3. Moderate effort
4. Strong effort
5. Intense effort

You can determine this by assessing his willingness, energy level, coordination, sweating response, and heart rate after 45 minutes of doing one of the following exercise combinations (performed as briskly as possible):

- Spiraling In and Out (page 38)
  Exercise on a Slope (page 59)
  Trotting Poles in an Arc (page 108)

- Waltzing with Your Horse (page 45)
  Changing Speeds (page 95)
  Exercise on a Slope (page 59)

- Cantering on Uneven Terrain (page 113)
  Gymnastic Jumping 1 (page 62)
  Loops and Poles (page 44)
  Gymnastic Jumping variation (page 63)

Signs to look for include the following:

Willingness

Observe your horse's attitude and behaviors from start to finish. Note small or seemingly unimportant things, which can be telling.

✓ Is the horse resistant at any point during the session? If so, at what point?

✓ Is he more resistant to travel and perform in one direction than the other?

✓ Does he respond immediately to your cues/aids for each exercise or is there a delay?

✓ Is he distracted or uninterested in his exercises; does he pay attention to you?

Energy Level

Determine how much energy your horse exerts to accomplish the routine.

✓ Is his energy level *consistent* throughout the 45 minutes?

✓ Does his energy "fade" at any portion of the workout?

✓ Does he get amped up or excited (a possible sign of workload being too much)?

✓ Does he have energy for some of the exercises but not others?

Coordination

Carefully note any changes in your horse's way of moving during and after one of the above exercise combinations.

✓ Does he begin to stumble during one of the exercises?

✓ Does one stifle or both ever slip?

✓ Is he lumbering around or does he feel light on his feet?

✓ Near the end of the workout, is he dragging his toes?

✓ Is he clunking into ground poles?

✓ Is he forging or interfering with his feet?

✓ If so, at what point during a session does this happen?

Evaluate Sweating Response

As horses become more fit, their ability to dissipate and regulate body heat improves. This means, among other things, that they become better at sweating. A fit horse should begin to sweat fairly early on in a work session (after approximately 15–20 minutes of actual work) and should sweat moderately — not profusely — as long as his work lasts.

On completion of a workout, his sweating should cease and his surface temperature should drop to normal within minutes. A horse that either doesn't sweat or sweats profusely lacks fitness or

HOW DOES YOUR HORSE SWEAT?

How much — and how frequently — your horse sweats is worth paying attention to, even if you are only a weekend rider. A fit horse ideally produces clear sweat over his entire body. Thick, foamy sweat, in contrast, indicates the presence of proteins in the sweat, which often means the horse is either under stress or overheated. Foamy sweat does not dissipate heat as efficiently as clear, runny sweat, which keeps the horse's underlying coat evenly moist while breezes and evaporation bring his overall temperature down.

Normal sweat contains salts that regulate a number of body processes such as pumping of the heart, moving of material through the gastrointestinal tract, and filtering wastes through the kidneys. When exercised in very hot, humid weather, horses can lose up to 30 teaspoons of salt in an hour. On the cellular level, these salts control fluid balances in the body by regulating movement of water in and out of cells.

Without a sufficient balance of circulating salts (through sweating and then replenishment), horses may weaken, fatigue, and fail to recover from even basic exercise. Therefore, you want to be sure your horse has a normal sweat response to exercise.

✓ Does he sweat all over or only in one area of his body?

✓ How long does it take for him to begin sweating when you ride?

✓ Does he stop sweating as soon as exercise stops? If not, he may be prone to overheating.

is demonstrating a metabolic shortcoming. (See page 12 for a more on sweat patterns.)

Determine Recovery Rate

Make a note of how the horse appears when you finish this assessment workout. Notice whether anything about his gait has changed (is he carrying his neck very low, dragging his hind toes back to the barn, or shortening his stride?). Watch to see whether he rests one or, alternately, both hind legs once returning to the cross-ties or to his stall.

Follow-up

Observe the horse the following day. This is critical! Does he seem fatigued, sore, unwilling in any way, irregular or stiff in his gait? Your notes will help determine the condition of his muscles and supporting structures.

After starting the horse into exercise based on the above assessment, recheck his cardio fitness and determined rate of exertion on the same exercises after 6 weeks to measure improvement.

What Does It Take to Get a Horse in Shape?

The horse's cardiovascular system adapts quite rapidly to conditioning compared with the much slower adaptations in the muscular and skeletal systems. In addition, it can take many more months for ligaments and tendons to acquire the same level of fitness exhibited by the cardiovascular

---

HOW TO MONITOR THE HEART RATE

An average mature riding horse has a resting pulse rate between 32 and 40 beats per minute when he is standing still and not exercising. Learn what your own horse's resting pulse rate is by taking it several times over the course of several days and averaging the results.

USING A STETHOSCOPE

To use your stethoscope, place the face of the chest piece on the horse's left chest wall in the girth area just behind and slightly above his point of elbow as shown. Allow the horse to get comfortable with it there (so his pulse rate is not mistakenly higher from worrying). Listen closely. Each "lub-dub" you hear is counted as one heartbeat. Count the lub-dubs for 15 seconds and then multiply by 4 for the total beats per minute.

Aerobically, it is most efficient for horses to exercise at a heart rate between 120 and 160 beats per minute. A well-conditioned horse's heart quickly drops back to his normal resting rate as soon as he stops working. Within 10 to 15 minutes of ending rigorous exercise, a horse's pulse rate should be near 60 beats per minute. After 20 to 30 minutes, it should return all the way to his resting rate.

TAKING THE PULSE

You can also take your horse's pulse by gently pressing with your fingertips on the arteries under his jaw, inside his knee, under his tail (several inches from the top), or on his pastern. Once you locate his pulse in one of these areas, count the beats as described above.

and muscular systems early on. Full conditioning of tendons and ligaments sometimes requires twice as much time as the muscular system. Even though a horse may look and act fit sooner, his

WHAT IS LACTIC ACID?

Most people have heard warnings about a substance called "lactic acid." As the lore goes, it builds up in your muscles and makes them burn, and eventually your muscles tire and give out because of it. But this isn't the whole picture. In a conditioned body, lactic acid is a *good* thing. It actually acts as a fuel, just like other energy sources in the body do.

Muscle cells convert glucose or glycogen into lactic acid and then burn it for energy. Specifically, lactic acid is absorbed and used as a fuel by mitochondria, the "energy factories" in muscle cells. Intense training causes muscles to adapt to absorb lactic acid more readily. Through conditioning, as the mass of muscle mitochondria increases, a body is able to more efficiently burn increased amounts of lactic acid, which allows the muscles to work harder and longer.

What about the old theory that lactic acid is bad? It is only "bad" (in that it leads to a burning or quivering sensation in the muscle, fatigue, and sluggish recovery) when body/muscle mitochondria have not been conditioned through appropriate training for the exercise at hand and, therefore, cannot absorb this metabolic waste as *fuel* for exercise. Instead, the acid pools in the tissue, causing inflammation and muscle fatigue. The same is true in the scenario of insufficient warm-ups and cooldowns.

When a conditioning program proceeds progressively and consistently, lactic acid is a natural part of the equation. If a program is rushed, too intense, or sporadic, lactic acid becomes an enemy.

bones and tendons may be quite far behind in their development.

A horse's age, breed, and conformation will determine at what level of intensity he can or should be worked. Some breeds take longer than others to develop an appreciable level of fitness. Generally speaking, though, 3 to 4 days a week of focused exercise will suffice for improving condition. Bear in mind that muscles need 48 or more hours to recover and rebuild after a workout; therefore, horses should not generally perform the same types of exercises on consecutive days to allow the time for repair of minor tissue damage.

With changes involving soft tissue, riders *must* remember that progress takes time. Riders are often in a hurry to see results from schooling and conditioning and, while outwardly the horse may seem to be progressing along quickly, he will soon hit a plateau or even a roadblock (such as sustaining an injury or developing a poor attitude) if the training schedule is too rushed.

Especially if you have either a young horse or a horse that is new to you or your chosen discipline/training methods, give yourself a full year to allow his body its necessary structural adaptations. I recognize that a year may seem like a long time, but it honestly takes that long to recondition the horse's skeletal muscles as well as strengthen the muscles that support them. Although change may indeed be initiated within that time frame, it takes *much* longer to make permanent changes in a horse whose posture muscles are being asked to engage in an entirely different way. Some of his muscles may show quick signs of strengthening and development, but his entire *system* will not necessarily be at the same level.

KEY POINT I've had clients send me horses for training hoping to see some kind of results within 30 or 60 days, but this is neither realistic nor reasonable. It can take up to 3 years of exercise with consistent intensity for a horse's entire physical body to reach its ultimate level of fitness.

Use Rest Wisely

Plan your weeks so that your horse's days off coincide with a rest between fairly active workouts to allow for the repair of minor tissue damage. In this way, you will get the most out of your schooling sessions. You do not need to "pound the pavement" every day to create a fit horse; you just need to use your time wisely. Productive schooling followed by a day of rest and then another active schooling/conditioning session the next day will accomplish much more than riding the same exercise multiple days in a row.

On days off, active rest is better than passive rest where the horse just stands around. Following a workout of any duration in which the horse was asked to utilize his musculature, lactic acid will accumulate as a result of fatigue. When a horse just stands around, the lactic acid can take up to a few days to flush from the tissues.

When a horse is longed lightly or hand walked or hacked at a gentle pace on his day off, however, the muscles are warmed up and utilize the lactic acid as an energy source, thereby fully flushing it out much more quickly. So, rather than resting your horse by allowing him to stand around passively, ensure that his "rest" days include activity where he moves around.

How Much Should I Work My Young Horse?

With regard to "rules" about conditioning, a horse's tolerable workload is influenced in large measure by his genetics. If he has a strong and athletic conformation, he will profit from early exercise even before three years of age. If he has deficiencies in his conformation, however, or appears to be maturing slowly, he will be able to tolerate only a lesser amount of exercise. Every horse is different genetically and, although there are general guidelines, some horses will do perfectly fine with exercise earlier in their careers and others will need to wait.

Tendons are at their most elastic state when a horse is under two years old. Research has shown that light exercise during these years will adapt his body to greater amounts of athletic output later in life by conditioning his tendons/ligaments while they are in their most flexible stage.

Your focus at this point should be on the following goals:

- Gaining the youngster's complete and total relaxation and confidence when being handled so that he stays calm and breathes deeply
- Teaching him to carry his body straight while traveling
- Providing him with as much turnout as possible, preferably with companions of the same age to play with
- Working him on very large longe circles (at least 60 feet [18 m] in diameter, for no more than 20 minutes at a time) on uneven terrain to increase proprioception and coordination

All the stretches and massages in this book are good for a young horse; other suitable exercises include ponying on trails behind an older experienced horse, hand walking on hills, and ground driving in straight lines. Handle him at least three days per week; by the end of the two-year-old year, many horses can be ridden lightly at least at a walk for 20 minutes at a time.

Situations to avoid include demanding a particular frame or posture in his body; repetitive circling, such as in a round pen, which damages bones forming in his feet and produces too much torque in his legs; and long sessions that go beyond his mental stamina.

Conditioning the Three-Year-Old Horse

For many years, the general rule of thumb handed down by trainers was, "ride a three-year-old three times a week, a four-year-old four times a week, and a five-year-old five days a week." Most trainers, however, now realize that, although this rule does hold true in many cases, much depends on the maturity and physical development of the individual horse.

Some three-year-olds, especially warmblood breeds, are not physically developed enough to be ridden above a walk. What some owners fail to realize is that the growth plates in the horse's back are the last ones to close; therefore, his skeleton and supporting soft tissue are quite susceptible to

TIPS FOR THE THREE-YEAR-OLD

The skeleton is still forming at this point, but the horse will respond to exercise positively without the same risk of injury as in his earlier years. Week by week, you can add slightly more to his conditioning program to prepare him for an injury-free career. When a three- or four-year-old is newly under saddle, you should ride him only about 25 minutes per session, riding him in slow tempos that don't stress his body. If he is unbalanced in the canter, avoid it for now.

Every month, increase overall riding time by 5 minutes and, after 3 months, begin to canter a little bit in both directions every session (think 2–3 minutes of total cantering to be done in large circles and on straightaways). The best exercises for a horse this age are:

- Moderate arena riding
- Trail riding at a distance of 4 miles (6.5 km) — preferably at a walk
- Short periods of work over ground poles to develop coordination
- Overall cardiovascular conditioning
- Exercises to build and strengthen the topline

Things to avoid include jumping; repetitive work on consecutive days; working to the point of exhaustion; undertaking multiple disciplines; riding longer than an hour at a time; and all sitting trot or riding with a deep seat in general.

permanent damage if required to bear the weight of a rider too early. You will need to make an honest assessment of your horse's physical development to determine whether he is suited for light riding a couple of days a week in his three-year-old year. Some horses can handle this just fine, others cannot.

Today's show arenas are seeing increasing numbers of three-year-olds in competition, which means a certain amount of exercise and riding must be done to prepare them. However, riders and trainers *must* keep in mind that the horse's body during this year cannot withstand being forced into any particular posture for prolonged periods of time. His skeleton is still not completely formed, his joints are highly susceptible to long-term damage, and his muscle structures lack both the strength and metabolic function to handle serious athletic output.

The three-year-old year is best viewed as a foundation year during which to build the remainder of the horse's career and life. It is a year in which he increases both mental and physical stamina through progressively longer and more focused training sessions. It is also the crucial year in which he learns to work willingly, to trust his handlers, and to go through his paces without compromising the natural aptitude of his gaits.

In terms of fitness and performance, a three-year-old should not be expected to gain much strength. He can, however, increase his stamina and symmetrical balance. As a general rule, three-year-olds should be ridden only three days a week. Other exercise days might include longeing, turnout, or hand walking.

Conditioning the Four-Year-Old and Five-Year-Old Horse

In the four-year-old year, the horse's vertebral column is typically more formed and able to functionally carry a rider with consistency. In so doing, the skeleton can reasonably be asked to assume a particular posture that utilizes the ring of muscles. The increased mental maturity and perhaps more

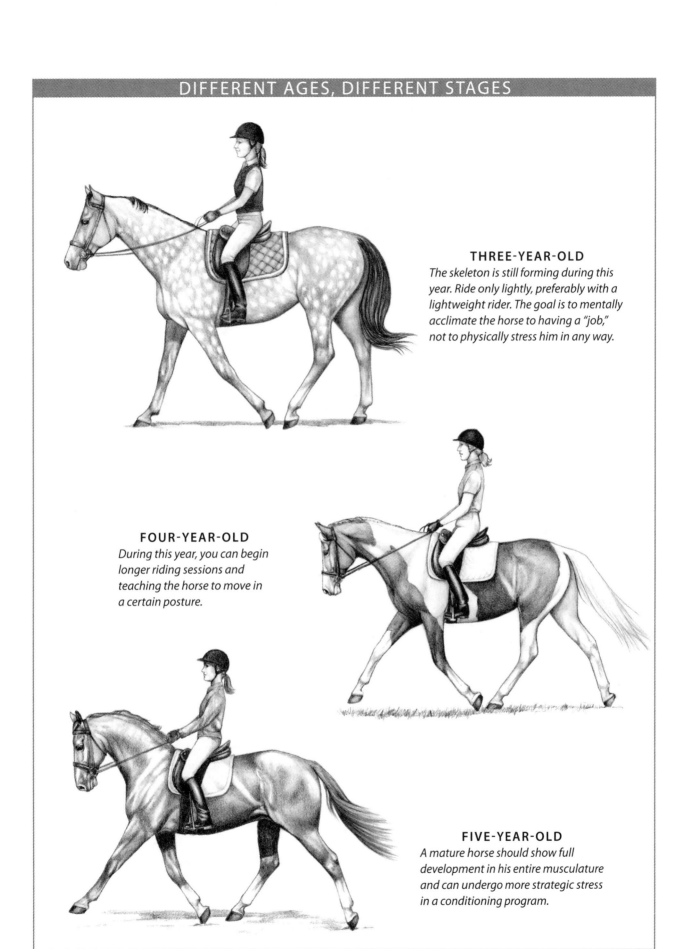

THREE-YEAR-OLD
The skeleton is still forming during this year. Ride only lightly, preferably with a lightweight rider. The goal is to mentally acclimate the horse to having a "job," not to physically stress him in any way.

FOUR-YEAR-OLD
During this year, you can begin longer riding sessions and teaching the horse to move in a certain posture.

FIVE-YEAR-OLD
A mature horse should show full development in his entire musculature and can undergo more strategic stress in a conditioning program.

willing attitude of a four-year-old horse, however, must not be taken as a sign that he is *physically* capable of undertaking strenuous work.

Any extreme flexion of the horse's neck, for example, must be avoided as his topline muscles have still not reached their maximum potential; therefore, the horse would respond to extreme flexions by tensing certain areas of his body while

compromising others. His working posture must assume a certain outline and tone, but the chosen posture must allow for his topline muscles to be engaged and loose, not strained. As a general rule, four-year-olds can comfortably handle four riding workouts weekly.

If the horse has been ridden consistently and properly as a three- and four-year-old, serious work can begin as a five-year-old. His body can be placed under stress — strategically — to achieve more advanced levels of performance and conditioning. He can be expected to recover more quickly from workouts and physical stress, and his muscles can be expected to reach their full strength. Once a horse has reached a solid base of conditioning as outlined above, he can be expected to enjoy at least a decade of productive and generally injury-free exercise until he reaches his senior years.

Maintaining Fitness in the Mature Athlete

A horse that has achieved a solid baseline of fitness can maintain that level with three to five days of basic riding for an hour or more per day each week. When necessary, short periods of down time of one or two months can be afforded to him following a couple of seasons of heavy workload, or when a rider's schedule mandates time off. When started back to work following these rest periods, he will reach a pinnacle of fitness much faster than a horse who never previously developed a solid baseline of conditioning.

Generally after short rest spells, a once-fit horse can reach total fitness again within six to eight weeks. Each time a horse is brought back into exercise following a layoff, however, always start with calisthenics only for one to two weeks, followed by topline strengthening exercises for another two weeks before plunging into other conditioning. (See pages 34–36 for a more detailed timeline of fitness.)

Take special note of the surface on which you ride. A loose, sandy surface can increase the inten-

---

TIPS FOR THE FOUR-YEAR-OLD

If the horse has already been under saddle the previous year, in his four-year-old year he should begin to understand rein contact with the rider. This means that the rider should skillfully guide him towards carrying his body and topline in a correct frame. This frame should not be forced or insisted upon; rather, steps should be taken day by day to increase a horse's mental and physical ability to carry himself with good posture.

In many breeds, the horse's joints are still not yet fully formed at this age. Therefore, avoid concussive type work like jumping, trotting downhill, extensive sitting trot, lateral movements, and so on.

- When riding in the arena, rest the four-year-old on a long rein at least every 15 minutes. Back muscles fatigue quickly when not yet fully developed.
- Aim for a 50/50 balance of arena schooling with cross-training (e.g. trails, ground poles, uneven terrain).
- If you ride four days per week, be sure that for two of those days, you do some sort of unmounted calisthenics prior to riding such as stretches, rein-backs, or longeing. This will help keep the horse's back muscles loose.
- A four-year-old with decent conditioning should be able to sustain 45 minutes of arena riding at walk, trot, and canter. Avoid sessions longer than that.

sity of a workout by up to 50 percent. The same is true of riding steep grades. Monitor the time and intensity of your riding in these cases and be sure it correlates with your horse's current fitness level. As mentioned, basic riding weekly will maintain a certain tone and stamina for each horse after some fitness is achieved. To *increase* fitness, however, the horse will need to be logically put under a bit more stress, by increasing the duration of workouts, incorporating exercises from this book, etc.

Mind Your Footing

The surface on which you train greatly affects your horse's performance, as well as potentially adding further strain. For example, when a forelimb hits the ground the impact force is carried in virtually a straight line through the foot, knee, and shoulder all the way up to the spine. A hard surface (one with less than 2 inches [5 cm] of soft, loose, sand-type footing) risks damage to bones, cartilage, and joints; too-deep footing, in contrast, may put excessive strain on tendons, ligaments, and muscles.

Furthermore, a loose, sandy surface, depending on depth, can double the intensity of exercise compared to that of harder surfaces. Used carefully, this can have strength-training benefits. If ridden on too long, however, such footing can create soreness and inflammation in the soft tissues.

The ideal footing is approximately 3 inches (7.5 cm) deep with good cushioning for the horse's limbs. Various materials can provide this footing, from wood chips to sand to composite mixtures, as long as it is stable for the horse and he can get good traction in it without straining.

KEY POINT The horse's skeleton, hooves, and ligaments don't reach full development and maturity in some cases until seven years of age; therefore, riding during the early years of any horse's career must focus on simple gymnastic work that conditions a horse and builds him up. Steer clear of any type of riding or work that places a serious level of stress on his muscular and skeletal systems.

Conditioning the Older Horse

Genetics and breed type dictate when an individual horse might be considered "senior," but typically the equine body begins to be affected by age after about 15 years. Some horses reach well into their twenties before showing effects of aging, which include changes in the teeth, muscle mass and elasticity, joints, and stamina.

Regardless of when the aging process fully hits, most horses will continue to have many more productive riding years. Physically and mentally, they will age much better if they continue to be exercised. In fact, exercise is arguably more, not less, important for the senior equine since it combats arthritis, muscle deterioration, and stiffness. A simple rule to follow for conditioning older horses is to increase warm-up time, decrease intensity and duration of exercise, and increase cooldown periods.

As the horse ages, his circulation slows down and his muscles start to lose elasticity. During the senior years, your primary goal should be combating stiffness and keeping your horse as limber as possible. The emphasis should shift to keeping the circulatory system in order, with actual sweat-inducing exercise becoming of secondary importance. Because of their decreased energy levels, senior horses do not require the same rigorous exercise as in their younger days, but it's important not to let your older equine become a "weekend warrior." Arguably more than other horses, seniors require *consistent* exercise and will be left very sore or stiff if ridden only once or twice a week.

A CASE IN POINT

My own senior horse, "Kitty," is an example of an older equine athlete who is still in fine service. At 24, she is not as spry as during her heyday as a competitive trail-riding athlete and dressage lesson horse, but she still shows a fair amount of vigor and pride. Daily exercise not only helps her feel well physically, but it noticeably bolsters her spirit. Kitty still perks up when she comes out of her stall for her daily ride.

Since she and I have had a reliable lifelong connection, maintaining focused interaction with her human every day is part of the daily routine that keeps her healthy. If I were to say, "Oh, she's too old to ride" and cease with our daily workouts, she would suffer mentally and, therefore, physically. On that note, I encourage readers to keep putting in time with their senior equine athletes.

Motion Is Lotion for Seniors

Because their energy levels are lower than those of younger horses, seniors don't tend to move around as much in turnout and, therefore, rely on their human friends for exercise. To keep their joints and soft tissue as loose and functional as possible, seniors benefit from frequent exercise, even just a 25-minute jaunt several times a week. A brisk 2–4 mile (3–6 km) walk down a relatively flat trail followed by several stretches and/or massage is a decent amount of exercise for maintaining condition in a horse that is showing signs of arthritis and diminished body tone. Here are some other pointers to keep in mind.

Don't Overdo It

Older horses should not be ridden every day and ideally they should carry only lightweight riders. Look for ground-work exercises to incorporate into their routine. Many of the exercises in this book can be adapted to perform by ground driving rather than riding. Examples include Rein-Backs (pages 56–57), Transitioning Downward (page 42), and Trotting Poles in an Arc (page 108).

Watch the Weather

Older horses are more susceptible to the affects of weather. Damp and cold weather, in particular, mandates that they be allowed more time to warm up and cooldown following workouts. With their less-efficient metabolisms, older horses need adequate time for their body temperatures to regulate. In cooler weather, consider riding with a blanket covering the kidneys and loins to ward off chill and stiffness in the hind limbs.

Take a Break

Older horses tire faster; they cannot be expected to maintain the same level of intensity for the same duration as their younger counterparts. Because their muscles have less stamina, they require frequent walk breaks during any riding session.

Cantering Is Okay

After a long phase of walking and loosening up in the arena, most older horses warm up best in the canter because it is less strenuous on the joints, ligaments, and feet than trotting. Cantering your horse with a light/slightly forward seat might be best for him.

Check His Legs

Many older horses develop wind-puffs and thickened tendons, and their hind legs may stock up with fluid if they stand still too long. This is all perfectly normal, but be sure to feel your senior horse's legs frequently and have a good knowledge of what is a normal amount of lumpiness for him.

That way, you'll be able to tell when the swelling is worse.

Teach Him Some Tricks

Senior horses often enjoy the light exercise and mental activity of learning simple tricks like Spanish Walk, stepping up on a stool, counting with hoof taps, and so on. Consider trying some "fun" types of training with your horse such as clicker training or natural horsemanship games on the ground — most horses enjoy the challenge of learning new things.

Consider Going Bitless

Older horses already know their jobs and how to carry themselves. They don't need the extra pressure of a bit on their temporomandibular joint (TMJ) and tongue. To keep his mouth and neck relaxed, try riding your senior citizen in a sidepull or bitless bridle.

What to Avoid

Jumping, extensive sitting trot, riding down steep hills, lateral work (if there is a hoof problem like ringbone or coffin rotation), and riding sessions longer than an hour.

Dealing with Arthritis

Most horses eventually develop arthritis, often in their hocks, fetlocks, or shoulders. For many, this demonstrates itself as a gait irregularity or stiffness in their movement. Generally, they will warm out of it within 15 minutes of gently warming up. In the early stages, a good "cure" for arthritis is continued exercise and movement, which keeps joints as lubricated as possible. Learn to recognize when your horse has progressed past his "normal" irregularity, however, and might be in need of joint supplements.

Pulling Their Weight (Not Quite)

The following exercise is a good workout for older horses. Dragging a lightweight object makes a physical demand on the horse without the stress

---

OPTIMAL EXERCISES FOR SENIOR HORSES

Use the following exercises to maintain fitness and conditioning in an older horse.

4. Legging Up (page 41)
6. TMJ Massage (page 43)
10. Rein-Back up a Hill (page 56)
11. Rein-Back on a Curve (page 57)
12. Turn on the Forehand in Motion (page 58)
20. Tail Pull (page 74)
21. Tail Rotations (page 75)
38. Pick-up Sticks (page 109)
39. Lifting the Hind Legs (page 110)
40. Bringing the Hind Legs Forward (page 111)
42. Cantering on Uneven Terrain (page 113) — keep it gentle!
43. In and Out Leg-Yielding (page 114)
45. Rear-Leg Circles (page 119)
46. Pelvis Tuck (page 120)
49. Shoulder Circles (page 123)

---

of bearing weight on his back. *Your horse must be comfortable with ropes touching his back legs, noise behind him, and a breast collar before you attempt this!*

Outfit your horse with a breast collar and pulling traces (from a driving harness), snaffle bridle, and ground-driving lines. Attach the traces to an old tire, letting it drag about 3 feet (1 m) behind your horse's hind legs. Ground drive around an arena — or your property — at a walk; the tire will swing around too much at a trot. To make it more strenuous, have your horse pull the tire around various patterns such as serpentines and figure eights.

Once your horse is comfortably pulling around a tire, think of other ways to use this kind of exercise around your facility, such as pulling hay in a sled or clearing brush. Senior horses can be useful resources around a farm while simultaneously getting the exercise they need!

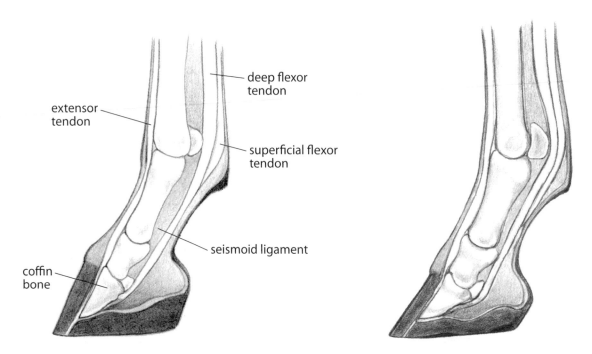

deep flexor tendon

extensor tendon

superficial flexor tendon

seismoid ligament

coffin bone

A hoof with too much heel pushes the coffin bone forward and down, which strains the tendons and ligaments and is bad for the legs.

The bones in a horse's leg will remodel based on the alignment of the hoof capsule. This can happen as swiftly as within six weeks.

No Foot, No Horse

A horse's whole performance relies on healthy, well-balanced feet. Hoof structure and health, to some extent, determine the amount of strain or tension on the lower leg tendons and ligaments. When a horse has unhealthy feet or improper hoof angles, his movement is sadly compromised. Without the ability to move forward fluidly and regularly, his body suffers and various shortcomings will occur, ranging from stiffened hips and tight shoulders to actual irregularities in the gait.

At this point, no matter how good the horse's training, he will plateau — or break down entirely — unless the state of his feet is addressed. This is analogous to a human going through her daily motions with a sore heel or injured toe. Her movement will be altered as she continues to move in a compromised manner. Because of this, her body will form specific ailments such as a shorter stride with one leg and a resulting painful knee or dropped shoulder.

Proper Alignment Is Crucial

Without properly aligned feet, a performance horse cannot move functionally and, therefore, cannot develop the right musculature. Over the past 30 years, it has become fashionable for farriers to leave longer heels on horses and rasp their toes. But this has the effect of pushing the horse's coffin bone forward inside the hoof capsule, maximizing pressure on the sole and straining the tendon/ligament system in the lower leg and foot. The thin dermis layer between sole and coffin bone is squished, the sole loses its arched "cup" around the frog, and the heel loses all rotation and flexibility. The horse's fetlocks and knees lose their shock absorber.

Scientific research and dissections over the last 20 years by Michael Savoldi, chairman of the American Farrier's Association equine research committee, has shown that the horse's coffin bone will remodel based on how the sole lies, determined by trimming and shoeing. Without a sole that assists in aligning the interior of the horse's foot, the horse's behavior and movement will alter as bones remodel and he experiences discomfort, mineralization, and lack of coordination.

This misalignment causes his entire posture to deteriorate and he will develop incorrect musculature or fail to fill out at all. Because of the mechanics involved, a faltering or incorrect gait prevents him from using his body fully. He may begin toe flicking, dragging a toe, locking a stifle, and so on. In his stride, he will land incorrectly, with the toe first instead of the heel first. He won't be able to extend his forelimb beyond his knee, he may pronate his hind legs, and he will most likely be either choppy or lethargic to ride.

As a brief example, if the hoof cannot rotate freely with ample heel flexion, a horse will develop very tight shoulder muscles and overdevelopment at the base of his neck. With the front end restricted like this, it is physically impossible for his hindquarters to come farther under his body. In addition, if the horse tries repeatedly to engage himself with a compromised front end, he will strain the compensating muscles, creating back pain or even tearing ligaments in the lower limbs.

What about the Barefoot Horse?

There are numerous opinions about the merits of leaving horses barefoot versus shoeing them. When a horse is barefoot, his heels are able to flex better with each stride and the hoof capsule itself is able to expand and contract on impact with the ground. This promotes better blood flow and a more natural wear and tear on the hoof, and some people argue that it allows for proper alignment of the bones within the hoof. Shoes, on the other hand, are thought to restrict this flexion and blood flow, which stresses the hoof capsule as well as the lower limb.

Without choosing a particular stance on barefoot versus shoes, I encourage riders to do a lot more research on their horses' feet. Every horse is different. Some naturally grow longer heels. Some grow hoof at a faster rate from month to

month. Others have crooked legs and therefore crooked feet.

The important thing is to work with your farrier to ensure that your horse is not trimmed just to achieve a textbook angle that is not designed to meet his needs and individual hoof characteristics. Each individual horse's feet must be aligned for him specifically, determined by how his angles are responding or remodeling monthly based on changes in his coffin bone.

> **KEY POINT** If a horse's feet are out of balance, no amount of good training and conditioning will improve his muscular development and performance, because he is incapable of using his whole body well. Rather than fill out, his musculature will remain braced and not gain condition.

The Importance of Consistent Exercise

The old saying "Motion is lotion" is perfectly applicable to equine fitness. Without a doubt, one of the best practices in developing an equine athlete is *consistency*. Sometimes what riders lack in consistency, they try to make up for with intensity. Unfortunately, if you work your horse rigorously just 2 days a week and let him stand around the rest of the time, all that you're doing is creating soreness. It is better to have more frequent sessions, even if they are shorter and less intense.

Regularity of workouts ensures circulation, nourishment of muscles, and flushing out of waste materials. Consistent movement means the horse is less prone to stiffness, deteriorated aerobic fitness, and stagnant metabolic processes. If you are forced to choose, or short on time, four 25-minute workouts are better than two 1-hour rides per week in terms of keeping the horse most suited for performance.

It's also important to maintain the same level of intensity throughout each daily session from start to finish. In other words, don't begin a session with a focused attitude and high expectations for the horse and then change tactics midway through. Not only is this approach unfair and confusing for the horse, it does not require an appreciable amount of work from the same muscle groups. When a different aerobic capacity and muscle function are required throughout a session, nothing in the horse's system is taxed long or hard enough to gain in fitness. What's needed is a focused, sustained level of exercise from start to finish (excluding, of course, the warm-up and cooldown phases). Note that this doesn't mean that you have to work at the same level of intensity every day. As long as you are consistent within each session, you can vary the intensity from day to day.

> **KEY POINT** As you tackle the conditioning exercises provided in this book, expect a high level of performance from your horse on each repetition and hold yourself accountable to help him achieve it. Remember, fitness is never improved by aimless exercise!

Staying Focused

Finally, stick to a plan. In your schooling and conditioning sessions, do not alternate among different training styles or disciplines (the exception here is cross-training between arena riding and riding outside on trails or cross-country). Using different methods or trainers with opposing approaches requires different postures and levels of engagement from your horse day to day. Constantly varying the program does not allow the horse to benefit from the regular targeting of specific muscle groups, balance, and symmetry. His body does not have the necessary time and consistency to adapt to a single, focused conditioning approach.

No Such Thing as Too Much Turnout

The exception to the rule "Shorter, more frequent workouts are better" is if your horse lives entirely

on pasture and is active throughout the day. Most horses, however, live primarily in confinement. In addition, we feed them concentrated feeds that stress their guts, which are already taxed from reduced physical movement and minimized forage intake. The combination predisposes them to colic, ulcers, and irregular energy levels, not to mention a range of behavioral stall vices — weaving, cribbing, sourness — that result from too much confinement.

A horse that lives in confinement is not able to build the same bone density or maintain the muscle looseness of a pastured horse. His legs and feet are more susceptible to injury from having to repeatedly go from a state of total rest to a state of active exercise. Stabled horses are more prone to splints, ligament strains, and damage within the hoof capsule. The more turnout, the better.

Given that many of us are unable to provide the optimal amount of turnout for our horses, here are some tips for keeping a stabled horse as healthy as possible:

- *Turnout.* Utilize whatever turnout options you have! One hour of turnout per day in a sandlot is better than none at all.
- *Movement.* Move your horse as much as possible throughout the day. For example, if you can, add an afternoon hand walk a few hours after you ride him in the morning.
- *Socializing.* Keep stabling situations social. Be sure your horse can at least touch noses with a neighboring horse for social interaction to encourage play and movement in his stall.
- *Feeding.* Feed your horse hay or other forage at least 3 times daily to mimic his natural grazing lifestyle. Minimize the amount of concentrated food he receives.
- *Warm-up.* Even if your horse is pent up from being in his stall, do not let him run as soon as he is on a longe line or turned loose in a paddock. Walk him or do controlled trotting for 10 minutes to warm up his legs before letting him blow off steam.

CHAPTER *3*

SCHOOLING VS. CONDITIONING

I LIKE TO SAY that the horse's muscular and skeletal systems — indeed his very makeup — are a network of pulleys and cables. With equine athletes, it is nearly impossible to isolate particular areas of the body or musculature for work. Trainers who believe otherwise have never studied equine anatomy.

The working of this musculoskeletal system depends on the smooth interconnected relationship of these pulleys and cables. As long as each part of the horse moves freely, the system works. But when a small glitch arises in any one pulley or cable, the *entire system* is affected. No part of the horse, regardless how remote the connection may seem to be, is independent from the rest.

Proper tone of individual muscle groups and ligaments happens because of nerves that control reflexes throughout the entire body. As an example, nerve centers in the spinal column at the top of the neck control reflexes that affect the posture of the entire body. When a horse's neck is correctly elevated in riding and training, his hindquarters automatically tuck underneath him as a result of these reflexes. These interdependent reflexes govern the horse's body position and carriage. In a nutshell, *how* a horse goes about his job determines whether he 1) becomes stronger and more fit from it, 2) receives no benefit from it, or 3) is ill affected by it.

Conditioning First, Schooling Second

The vast majority of horses hit training plateaus — failing strength in a particular area, lack of coordination, stiffness, resistance, unwillingness — for no other reason than a lack of fitness that inhibits them from performing certain exercises. For example, I have encountered several horses that do miles and miles of trail work weekly, but their bodies are not well toned. This is often because they are running down the roads in a crooked or hollow posture, and the reflexes between their interdependent muscle groups cannot react freely.

Instead of attaining better tone and fitness as they exercise, they become stiffer and tighter. I also see dressage horses that are ridden with their toplines very round for 40 minutes every day and yet their backs are still not strong. The reason is that the horse's neck muscles are too tight and pulling the withers down instead of up. The back is, therefore, flat or dropped rather than stretched properly.

Without overall fitness, a horse will fail to perform past a certain level. Even the recreational horse is a victim. Because of their busy schedules, some of my adult students ride only once or twice a week. This is fine, but occasional riders need to accept that they cannot expect the horse's performance level to increase with only two workouts per week. We would not expect ourselves to be totally functional athletes with that little amount of exercise per week and we cannot expect it of our horses. Instead, we must aim to make them stronger and more supple for their jobs, regardless of the discipline.

As modern training has become more specialized and discipline specific, it has often neglected the interdependent nature of the horse's musculoskeletal structure. Where this is the case, the horse's movement can never be optimally developed. In many cases, too much time in daily schooling is spent asking the horse to move through a predetermined set of exercises with his body in the same posture so that he maintains a certain "look" or frame. This type of training approach addresses and works only a small percentage of the horse's body and will never improve a horse's overall way of going or general condition.

Another consideration is that, just as their human counterparts, performance horses more often than not approach their exercise with a little stiffness in one limb, asymmetry in their balance, or a lack of smoothness to their gait. With cumulative exercise, rather than becoming stronger and developing more beautiful movement, their way of going actually deteriorates and their performance never measurably improves.

Too many riders do not execute their schooling with this in mind. I understand that there is already a *lot* to think about when riding a horse day-to-day in terms of our own seat and aids. But we owe it to our mounts to improve their bodies and their overall condition. Your horse must be conditioned first and schooled second.

KEY POINT It is especially true with quadrupeds that each individual part of the body affects the entire animal. Each muscle group must coordinate with all other muscle groups and ligaments to enhance the overall working of the horse.

Hip Bone Connected to the Thigh Bone

The drawing on the next page shows a general guideline for the interdependence of the horse's musculoskeletal system. Imagine what happens to the pulleys and cables in the diagram when the horse, for example, lowers his neck a few inches or pulls his hind legs up under his belly. Picture where the cables would be tighter and where they would have more slack. Now imagine the horse trotting. You'll recognize that, for a smooth gait, those cables would need to move very freely!

As you can see from looking at the drawing, any little "sticky" place results in the surrounding muscles gradually becoming more rigid and, over time, losing their suppleness altogether. At this point, regardless of the best intentions for conditioning and training, the horse will not become stronger for his job at hand because oxygen and blood flow to that particular muscle group will be reduced and the horse will not be using his entire body evenly — his movement will be compromised.

What often happens at this point is that the horse develops a subtle irregularity in his gait or suddenly displays an "unexplained" injury. When a shoulder muscle tightens from the horse being ridden in a compressed or hollowed neck frame, for example, it puts strain on the surrounding large ligaments and then down farther into the

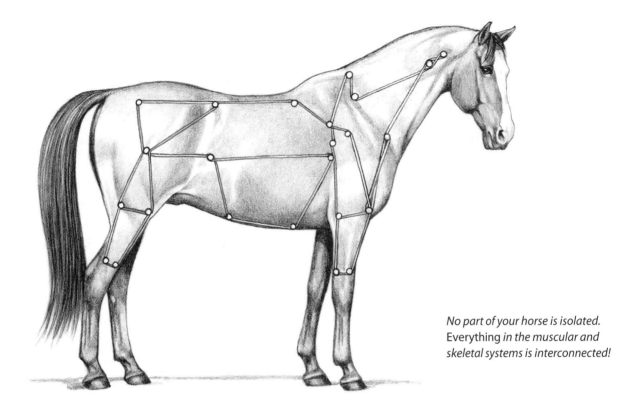

No part of your horse is isolated. Everything in the muscular and skeletal systems is interconnected!

smaller ligaments of the horse's leg, such as the suspensory ligament, until finally something tears. Sometimes these types of injuries are viewed and diagnosed as isolated malfunctions. It is crucial, however, to see that they are often brought on by lack of function in a nearby larger muscle group or in an area of the body even farther away. Because of this interconnectedness, the actual injury typically occurs at the weakest point, often the thinner ligaments located a fair distance from the compromised muscle group.

This helps explain why a horse undergoing rehabilitation for an initial injury may seem sound in the originally injured area while suddenly showing soreness or discomfort in a seemingly unrelated area. Or an injury can appear to move around from one spot on Tuesday to a totally different one on Thursday. It's the same when a human injures her knee and hobbles around trying to keep weight off that leg. In the meantime, she strains other areas of her body and develops a sore back or an achy hip. Then, while she's try-

ing to ease that area, she tightens a calf muscle or hamstring. The interdependence between muscles and the skeletal system has a cumulative effect on horses as well.

The Importance of the Jaw

A key example of the interconnectedness of the horse's motion and anatomy is the effect of his jaw on the rest of his movement. Sadly, many riders never consider this. They tighten their flash nosebands, cinch up curb chains, and ride with unsteady hands without giving it another thought. In nature, the horse's tongue would move freely in his mouth for up to 17 hours per day as he foraged in the wild. His jaw would move and chew throughout the day, rather than being motionless for hours on end. The corresponding muscles at the top of the skull and along the bottom of the neck would remain loose. With the domestication of horses, however, this has changed dramatically.

Not only do most modern horses not forage throughout the day, the ways in which we ride and train them often greatly compromise the freedom of their jaws, which in turn affects how they are able to carry and use their bodies. When a horse feels excessive pressure from the bit or an overly tight noseband and is forced against his natural instinct to keep his tongue/jaw still, especially during early years of training, he responds by bracing his lower jawbone — the mandible — upward. That action puts strain and pressure on the horse's temporomandibular joint mechanism near the top of his skull. This pattern of bracing spreads throughout the horse's entire musculoskeletal system.

KEY POINT

For a horse to reach the pinnacle of performance, his entire structure must function loosely and harmoniously during his daily exercise.

Try this on yourself: walk or jog while tightly clenching your jaw. How does this affect the rest of your body? It tightens the back of your neck, your shoulders pinch upward, and your stride shortens. It has the same effect on your horse. If a significant amount of mental and physical effort is invested in bracing the mandible, how well can the horse move?

Working for long periods of time in this compromised state will break your horse down. While a visible lameness may never occur, the horse can only perform with stiffness. Biomechanically, the hindquarters cannot come under the body unless the front end moves freely and softly, which it does not in this scenario. This is the breaking point of most performance training.

TIPS FOR KEEPING YOUR HORSE'S JAW LOOSE

- Feed on the ground, not from a raised feeder
- As much as possible, feed hay rather than pellets or cubed hay products, which reduce a horse's eating and chewing time
- If your horse lives inside rather than on pasture grazing, give him several (at least three) forage feedings throughout the day
- Allow your horse social interaction so he can groom and nuzzle other horses with his mouth
- Make sure your bit allows the horse's tongue to move; many bits are too thick and cause too much pressure in the mouth
- Do not tighten your noseband so much that it restricts mobility in the jaw

Tension in the jaw spreads to the neck and throughout the body.

Fitness Timeline

These guidelines are intended for an average riding horse, aged 3 to 15 years old, who has been out of consistent exercise for a prolonged period of time. Every conditioning program should start with exercises that put no weight on the horse's back. Begin with at least 2 weeks of calisthenics (pelvis tucks, backing up hills, tail pulls, stretches, and so on) for about 10 to 15 minutes every other day, along with a program of ample turnout, longeing, round-pen work, or ground driving.

After a couple of weeks, you can begin with 25-minute riding sessions. After 10 days of short riding sessions, add two of the simpler exercises from this book to your routine. Here are some good ones:

1. Spiraling In and Out (page 38)
3. Strengthening the Front End (page 40)
10. Rein-Back up a Hill (page 56)
11. Rein-Back on a Curve (page 57)
30. Horizontal Frame Conditioning (page 94)
38. Pick-up Sticks (page 109)

Continue like this, in intervals of 10 days, making your sessions increasingly more difficult in terms of duration or intensity. At the end of each month, inventory your progress to determine whether you need to back off or you are building condition.

There are some questions to ask as you assess your progress:

✓ Where — in what areas — is your horse's muscling filling out?

✓ Has he developed resistance to you or to his work? Has anything about his attitude/behavior changed?

✓ Does he start out stiff each day, indicating that he's not recovering well from the previous day?

✓ Does he "fade" partway through your sessions (e.g., faltering steps, fatiguing, delayed response to cues, loss of gait quality)?

✓ Is he losing too much weight? Or is he not shedding fatty deposits?

Having a regular check-in with your horse will help you determine where in his conditioning you might need to back off, plateau for a while, or add intensity. Do *not* increase intensity if your horse has not acclimated to the previous few weeks' demands. If his musculature, strength, and energy levels have not increased, you will not improve or

accelerate his conditioning by making his program harder. You may need to add more calisthenics for a short period before moving on.

Breaking Your Program into Phases

I like to think of a conditioning program as including a few different phases. Handled correctly, these phases flow seamlessly together provided that neither horse nor rider suffers prolonged illness, injury, or time off.

Preparatory Phase (1–2 months)

This phase of ground work only is spent preparing the horse's topline and back muscles with calisthenics and stretching. Plan to work the horse at least 3 days per week. At this point, you will not "see" measurable results in your horse's overall performance level (stamina, strength, quality of movement). You should, however, note some weight loss and muscle gain. Also, the horse will benefit from this period of consistency of mental and physical demands. Some exercises that are useful in this phase are:

7. Loops and Poles (page 44)
10. Rein-Back up a Hill (page 56)
11. Rein-Back on a Curve (page 57)
12. Turn on the Forehand in Motion (page 58)
18. Double Longe (page 66)
19. Arena Interval Training (page 68)
20. Tail Pull (page 74)
25. Loosening the Back (page 82)
30. Horizontal Frame Conditioning (page 94)
31. Changing Speeds (page 95)
38. Pick-up Sticks (page 109)
46. Pelvis Tucks (page 120)

Basic Cardio Phase (1 month on average, but can take up to 3 months)

The next stage is adapting the horse's respiratory and muscular systems to daily exercise, with no emphasis on strength training yet. Your goal is to build stamina, improve recovery time, sharpen the horse's mental focus, and, if needed, lose body fat while building up overall tone. Plan to work the horse 4 or 5 days per week and stagger his days off; do not clump them together.

At the end of this phase, be sure that your horse can carry himself properly in the correct posture as described in chapter 4. Moving on to the next phase before this is the case will not improve strength and conditioning. Here are some good exercises for this phase:

2. Sprint Lines (page 39)
13. Exercise on a Slope (page 59)
16. Gymnastic Jumping (page 62)
19. Arena Interval Training (page 68)
31. Changing Speeds (page 95)
37. Trotting Poles in an Arc (page 108)

Strength-Building Phase (2 months)

By now, you should be spending 2 or 3 days per week schooling for your particular discipline and 1 day working on cardio-fitness maintenance. Now add 2 days of strength training with exercises from this book that tax the horse's coordination, impulsion, and joint flexion such as:

5. Transitioning Downward (page 42)
13. Exercise on a Slope (page 59)
14. Riding a Drop (page 60)
15. Canter to Walk Downhill (page 61)
34. Shoulder-In Repetitions (page 99)
37. Trotting Poles in an Arc (page 108)
41. Stepping Over Slowly (page 112)
42. Cantering on Uneven Terrain (page 113)

Maintenance

From here on, your horse will maintain a solid level of fitness with regular riding. Remember that 50 percent of his weekly work should consist of schooling for his particular discipline and the other 50 percent should consist of calisthenics and fitness exercises from this book. Ideally you'll continue to work 4 or 5 days a week. If that is not possible, aim for a consistent routine of every other day. A minimum of 3 days is necessary to keep baseline fitness. The following exercises work well in this phase:

9. Gearing Up to Gallop (page 46)
10. Rein-Back up a Hill (page 56)
11. Rein-Back on a Curve (page 57)
13. Exercise on a Slope (page 59)
14. Riding a Drop (page 60)
16. Gymnastic Jumping (page 62)
32. Counter Canter Loops (page 97)
33. Counter Canter Serpentines (page 98)
36. Striding In, Striding Out (page 101)
42. Cantering on Uneven Terrain (page 113)

1. Spiraling In and Out 38

2. Sprint Lines 39

3. Strengthening the Front End 40

4. Legging Up 41

5. Transitioning Downward 42

6. Temporomandibular Joint (TMJ) Massage 43

7. Loops and Poles (David Lichman) 44

8. Waltzing with Your Horse (Sherry Ackerman) 45

9. Gearing Up to Gallop (Yvonne Barteau) 46

CONDITIONING EXERCISES

1. Spiraling In and Out

Don't be fooled by this deceptively simple-seeming exercise, which is so useful it could be incorporated into every schooling session. This work strengthens your horse by making him more supple and better balanced, therefore making his muscular system looser and more elastic. This will help keep him in top form. Remember, a supple horse is a more symmetrical horse and a symmetrical horse is a more functional horse!

How Do I Do This?

1. Begin in an active working trot rising on a big circle, 20 meters or larger.

2. After a few revolutions around the circle to ensure you are maintaining a steady and rhythmic trot, begin to shrink the circle down to as small as possible without losing tempo or balance.

3. With each stride, ask him to move over a little more until your circle gets smaller and smaller. You will most likely be on a circle about 10 or 12 meters in diameter.

4. After two revolutions around the small circle, begin to guide your horse one step at a time out to the larger circle you started on.

5. Repeat the exercise twice in each direction.

TIPS FOR SUCCESS: When enlarging the spiral, use your aids this way: when you are rising up out of the saddle, nudge the horse sideways in that instant with your inside leg at the girth. Take approximately three revolutions to end up back on the larger circle.

While you are moving to the larger circle, be sure you keep your horse's spine evenly bent from poll to tail toward the inside of the circle.

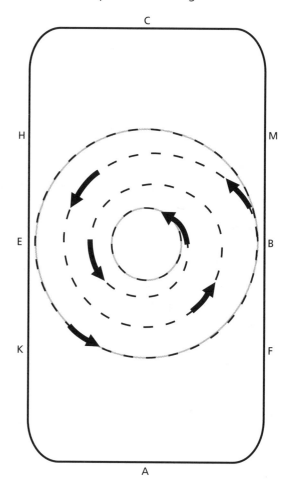

2. Sprint Lines

This fun routine is an abbreviated version of time-tested and successful interval training. It creates a physically intense training session in a relatively short period of time. The swift bursts of energy improve a horse's cardiovascular response as well as build his propulsive muscles — the ones responsible for power and acceleration.

In a large arena or other open flat area, set up several small cones or other markers in a big oval as shown. Use your horse's stride length to set the distances, going from just two or three strides to as many as ten. The exact distances between the cones aren't as important as having them vary between each one. You want to develop your horse's overall muscle power and lung capacity by mixing up the shorter and longer distances each time.

How Do I Do This?

1. Develop a nice working canter that is rhythmic and balanced.

2. As you approach the first cone, pick up an extended canter and sprint to the second cone.

3. Immediately after you pass the second cone, slow down to your original working canter.

4. After passing the third cone, sprint forward to the fourth cone and return to the slower working canter at the fifth one.

5. Continue like this for 5 minutes, then take a 5-minute walk break and repeat the pattern for another 5 minutes.

6. Do this three times in each direction.

TIPS FOR SUCCESS: The *quality* of this exercise is what counts! The most important aspect is the speed intervals, but you must also pay attention to how your horse uses his body. Make sure he remains balanced and round with his ring of muscles.

You may want to first practice the exercise Transitioning Downward (page 42) for a few moments to get him listening to your seat and cues.

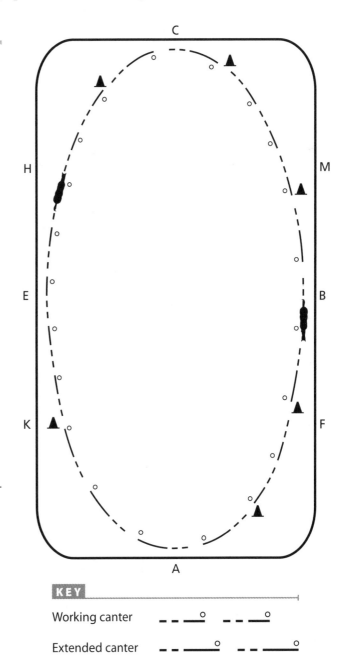

KEY	
Working canter	
Extended canter	

3. Strengthening the Front End

Forehand muscles and ligaments do not receive enough stress for gymnastic development in routine flat work, leaving the muscles of the forehand weak and prone to strain. These mechanisms only become stronger and more elastic when strategically stressed with a repetitive intensity such as galloping and riding on uneven terrain. The correct intensity goes beyond brief moments of cantering in the arena to long, sustained periods of galloping outside on open land where the horse can really move out.

Many riders, especially arena riders, hesitate to gallop their horses for fear that the horse will become excited and difficult to handle; however, once a horse learns that the gallop — as everything else — is just another exercise to be performed to a certain level of fatigue, rather than an isolated and exciting experience, he will approach it with much less excitement.

How Do I Do This?

1. If you are not accustomed to riding your horse outside the arena, begin by *walking* your horse at a brisk pace on open terrain. Don't walk him as though there are scary "bogeymen" in the bushes, but as though you have a long distance to cover in a short time. Remember, this is a workout, not a stroll. Teach him to stay focused and marching along on all kinds of terrain. Once you have relaxation at the walk, you are ready for the gallop.

2. Begin with a 1-mile (2 km) gallop but not on overly steep terrain. Rolling ground is fine, as are gentle slopes. Practice this once a week. If you have access to more mileage/land, you may want to ride a longer gallop every couple of weeks, up to 3 miles (5 km).

3. Maintain a gallop for a *sustained* period of time. Do not, for instance, gallop up a short hill and then break back to a trot. These short bursts will only excite the horse and do nothing to provide the continuous stress he needs to build a stronger front end to prevent ligament strain in future work. Allow the horse to settle into his gallop and maintain it.

TIP FOR SUCCESS: Practice the gallop on different leads each time to be sure you're riding the horse symmetrically.

Ride with a light seat, with your weight slightly inclined forward, so the horse's back is entirely free to undulate and to draw his hind legs forward in big strides.

4. Legging Up

"Legging up" is the practice of walking a horse on hard ground or pavement for 20+ minutes a couple of times per week either in hand or under saddle. Walking (without the concussion that is incurred by trotting) on hard ground is believed to tighten the lower leg tendons and strengthen the horse's legs overall. The practice has been used for decades for performance horses in various disciplines.

Keeping his legs fit by keeping his tendons and ligaments as tight as possible is a surefire way to keep him in service. A horse has no muscles below his knee; the area is entirely bone and supporting tissue (tendon, cartilage, and ligament). To keep this area as "tight" as possible, it can be useful to stress it slightly and then allow it to recover.

How Do I Do This?

1. Find an area that is mostly flat. Terrain with too much slope requires the horse to constantly adjust his stride. You want the horse to develop a steady rhythm and stride length (analogous to a human bicyclist being able to remain in one gear and pedal evenly for a stretch).

Pavement is desirable, but packed dirt works well, too. Most boarding stables have a large parking area or roadway to suit the purpose.

2. Strive for a brisk, active walk with purpose where the horse is actively rolling his feet forward with each stride. Remember that you are trying to create a gentle concussion to lightly stress the horse's legs. To achieve this, the horse should travel at a lively pace. If riding, leave the horse on a loose rein, so he can carry his body in a relaxed and natural posture.

3. Walk for 1 or 2 miles (2–3 km), which equals about 12–20 minutes.

TIPS FOR SUCCESS: A good rule is to ride your horse in the morning, cool him out, and let him rest a few hours. Then, in the afternoon, do 20 minutes of legging up.

Space legging-up sessions at least 2 days apart; 3 or 4 days is fine.

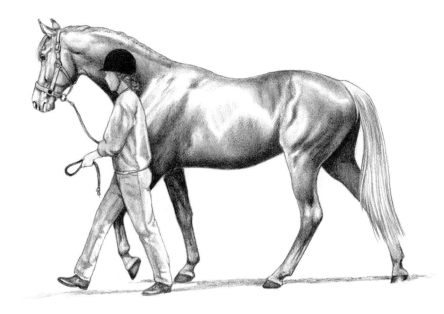

5. Transitioning Downward

Notice that this exercise is called "transitioning," rather than simply "transition." This is to stress the importance of making the gait change *gradual* and smooth as opposed to sharp and abrupt. A prompt but poorly postured transition does nothing but confirm bad postural habits for the horse.

In gradually downshifting from the trot before walking, the horse keeps his hind legs pulled under his body, which causes them to bear more weight in the moment of the transition. If the rider were to make the transition too abrupt, the horse would leave his pelvis and hind legs out behind him, which would weaken him. The strengthening benefit comes from *how* this simple exercise is ridden.

How Do I Do This?

1. Begin in an active working trot, tracking to the right around the rail of the arena.

2. In the middle of the long side of the arena, when your horse's body is fully straight, transition down to a slower trot.

3. Proceed for three strides like this and adjust your posting to rise lower and closer to the saddle.

STEP 3

4. Then, from the slower trot, transition down to a walk, waiting to sit down fully onto your horse's back until the first complete stride of walk. During the transition, ensure that your horse reaches his nose out slightly so that his face is slightly ahead of the vertical.

5. Immediately energize the walk following the transition.

STEP 4

6. Practice in both directions.

STEP 5

TIPS FOR SUCCESS: Don't sit down too early when riding from trot to walk.

Continue posting until the very *last* stride of the trot so that your horse keeps his back lifted and round through the transition, rather than dropping it away from the rider's weight.

6. Temporomandibular Joint (TMJ) Massage

Gently massaging your horse's jaw muscles can help alleviate much of the discomfort and tightness that so many performance horses endure as a result of their highly structured lives. The muscle that controls the TMJ is responsible for opening and closing the mouth. Keeping your horse's TMJ relaxed and pain free will help keep his neck and back loose.

How Do I Do This?

1. With your horse relaxed on the cross-ties (or tied in his stall), gently stroke his jaw area.

2. When he accepts this rubbing, begin to make tiny circular motions with the pad of your first two fingers where his jaw muscle begins (a point made by intersecting a line straight down from the base of his ear and a line straight sideways from the center of his eye).

3. After several seconds of circling, hold direct firm pressure on this spot for several seconds and then release.

4. Move down 1 inch (2.5 cm) and begin tiny circles in a new spot. Then, apply direct pressure.

5. Move down 1 more inch (2.5 cm) and repeat.

TIPS FOR SUCCESS: Use the amount of pressure you would use to squish a grape.

This area can be surprisingly painful for many horses, so go slowly and use gentle circles rather than direct pressure if your horse is nervous. When in doubt, practice on yourself at the spot by your ear where lower and upper jaws come together.

STEPS 2 & 3

STEP 4

STEP 5

7. Loops and Poles

Contributed by David Lichman, Parelli Natural Horsemanship, 5-Star Professional (Specialty in Gaited Horses)

This is a coordination exercise that assists horses who are learning or struggling to keep a steady rhythm in their gaits; it is especially useful for gaited horses or those with irregularity to their strides.

To set up this exercise, mark out (or simply visualize) a five-loop serpentine on flat ground. Ideally, each loop should be no larger than 10 meters, although you can adjust the size according to how your horse responds. Set up a single ground pole at the beginning of each loop on the serpentine.

How Do I Do This?

1. Initially, ride each loop as a full circle.

2. Once you can negotiate the pattern with a steady rhythm, eliminate the circles and just ride the serpentine with poles. Remember to cross each pole in the center, not over the ends.

3. Cross directly over the center of each pole *after* changing your horse's bend for the new loop. The pole is intended to prevent him from rushing or falling into the new turn.

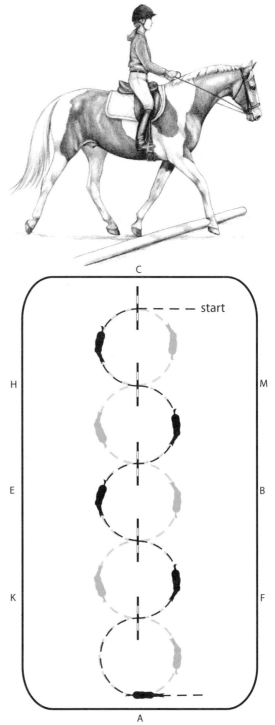

TIPS FOR SUCCESS: Ride the pattern at the walk until the horse is relaxed and steady, then advance to faster gaits. If you are not successful after two attempts at a faster speed, simply go back and practice at a walk until your horse is turning well around the loops.

If your horse seems tense or is bracing or becoming high headed, modify the serpentine to go twice (or more) around each circle from steps 1 and 2 above until your horse is staying more relaxed and soft.

It's best to do this pattern in a sitting trot so that your weight is deeply rooted in the saddle and your weight is not tipping forward, affecting the horse's balance. Most horses catch on to this exercise pretty quickly, although they may take some time to do it perfectly.

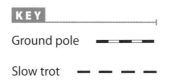

KEY	
Ground pole	▬ ▭ ▬
Slow trot	▬ ▬ ▬ ▬

8. Waltzing with Your Horse

Contributed by Dr. Sherry Ackerman, Author of *Dressage in the Fourth Dimension*

This exercise increases your horse's evenness from side to side by strengthening and stretching his oblique muscles, which support the loin and facilitate the horse's ability to lift his back. It is also beneficial for progressively strengthening the horse's haunches.

How Do I Do This?

1. Establish a brisk walk with contact on the straight side of the arena. Keep a steady rhythm. Sit so that your inside hip feels slightly more pushed down toward the ground than your outside hip and ask the horse to bend around your inside leg.

2. As the horse continues walking rhythmically forward, rotate *from the waist* so that your inside shoulder goes back while your outside shoulder goes forward. It is important that you rotate from the waist and not just move your shoulders.

3. Keeping your outside leg against the horse, allow him to bring his shoulders into a position that mirrors your shoulders.

4. Ride the movement for four strides and then straighten the horse and walk on.

5. Ride this exercise for 5 minutes in each direction.

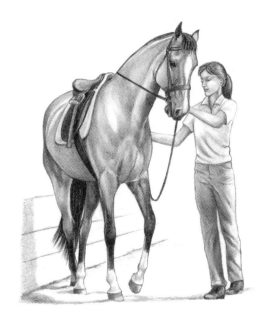

VARIATION

This exercise can also be done from the ground, which would be useful for a senior horse or one recovering from a layoff. In this case, the rider walks step for step in pace with the horse on the ground — like dancing with your horse!

1. Face your horse, holding a short whip toward his inside barrel to invite him to bend.

2. Bending and rotating from the waist, position your shoulders the same way you would in the saddle, allowing the horse to mirror the movement.

3. There should be a sense of gently and carefully drawing the horse's shoulders toward your body. Be careful not to interrupt the rhythm of the walk.

9. Gearing Up to Gallop

Contributed by **Yvonne Barteau,** FEI Trainer and Author of *Ride the Right Horse*

Riders who train primarily in the arena often fail to gallop their horses, thereby missing out on a really valuable tool for loosening their horses' backs and making overall movement freer and more expressive — enhancements to arena schooling! Galloping is vital for fitness as well as enhancing performance. Primarily, it helps the horse's back "let go" or loosen significantly. Then, his whole body is better off!

Define your comfort zone before you attempt this exercise. If you are afraid to gallop, you will not be a useful teammate for your horse. You *will*, however, be able to incrementally get past your fear one small step at a time.

How Do I Do This?

1. In an arena, develop a regular canter. Make sure you have a light rein contact and that the horse is in a rounded topline posture.

2. Then, for 30 seconds, make the canter bigger (slightly faster and with longer strides). Sit in either a deep seat or a half-seat, whichever makes you feel more secure.

3. Come back to a regular canter. Assess how well things went. Did your horse get excited? Were you confident and comfortable as a rider? Did the horse change his stride with what felt like more propulsive power? Did you maintain a good contact?

4. Again make the canter bigger for 30 seconds and return to a regular canter.

5. Alternate 30-second bouts of bigger canter with 30 seconds of normal canter. Keep doing this for several minutes.

6. Once you're adept and confident with the 30-second bouts, the next step is to stay in the bigger canter for longer than 30 seconds until it becomes a sustained period of galloping.

7. Eventually you will be ready to take your gallop outside the arena on open land, where you have more room.

TIPS FOR SUCCESS: In a bigger canter, the horse should *never* be out of control or overly excited. That's why we start in the arena — to show him how to do things appropriately. If your horse shows a tendency to get excited or out of control, stick with the 30-second bouts until he learns the drill!

This galloping movement is intended to free up the horse's back. Because of his larger strides, the horse will need to use his back in a manner very different from his usual way of going, so feel to see whether that is happening. You want longer strides, a feeling of a bigger jump with each stride, and a swifter tempo. Always remember to practice your 30-second bouts equally on both sides.

POSTURE DETERMINES STRENGTH

WHEN WE SPEAK OF STRENGTHENING a horse so that he moves better and lasts longer, we're talking about his ring of muscles. This ring of muscles determines, in large measure, whether the horse will advance in his training or plateau indefinitely. In any discipline, this ring of muscles is the alpha and omega. When he is in movement, these muscles should be engaged and supple, regardless of whether he is pulling a carriage, covering ground on a trail, or working cattle.

Most training plans would benefit from the old adage "Make haste slowly." When riders become eager to progress, they tend to skip steps, which too often means neglecting the basics. A rider might demand that her horse maintain a certain "look" or "frame" for the duration of his daily

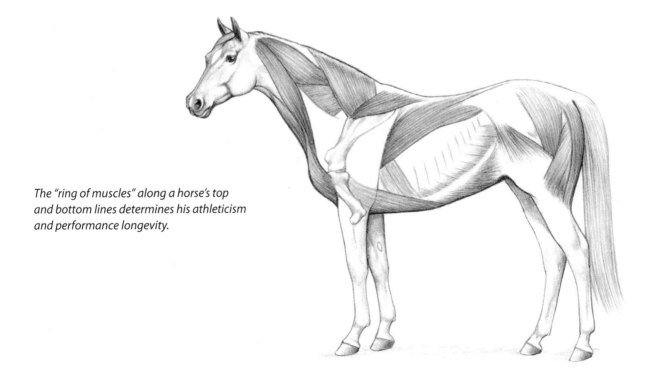

The "ring of muscles" along a horse's top and bottom lines determines his athleticism and performance longevity.

riding session even though that posture may create too much torque for an individual horse. Or she may ride her horse around the ring in no particular frame at all, allowing his muscular system to be slack and his posture bad. Remember that our horses cannot talk to us. We must learn what their bodies need because they cannot outright tell us!

Creating the Correct Posture

It is critical that a horse be strong and supple before he is asked to assume a particular frame. We can damage the horse's ability to perform by demanding an outline/posture before he is ready. Holding a posture incorrectly weakens his spine. The horse must be allowed to develop contact with the rider's hands over a long period as his balance and rhythm create a more sophisticated "open" frame with a long neck and not too much vertebral compression. Even when he is ready to be ridden with shorter reins, he should be worked in a collected frame for only brief periods of time. The majority

of riding, including trail riding, should be done on a gentle, light contact encouraging the horse to stretch his neck out long with the poll open and the nose in front of the vertical.

Working with light contact applies to ground work as well; therefore, I caution against auxiliary equipment such as draw reins that are thought to lift the horse's back and maintain a good posture. When a horse is worked with an overly rounded neck, his back must arch down for him to find his balance. The top neck muscles become too tense; the bottom neck muscles pull upward as the horse tries to support himself in this uncomfortable posture. This restricts respiration and blood supply. Initially, the horse's neck vertebrae will become stiff and tense. Continuing to work him in this manner will weaken his whole spine and result in unhealthy movement (resistance, choppy gaits, and hollow back).

Some riders, however, never ask *any* particular posture of their horses. These are the riders with excessively long reins who let their horses stick

This horse is working with proper posture, stretching his back, pushing nicely with his hind legs, and carrying his spine in a good balance.

The absence of any clear posture means that this horse is not moving in the most functional way possible. His belly muscles are sagging, which pulls his back down, and he is bearing most of his weight on his front legs.

their heads wherever they please — high or low. Although this may seem like the most "natural" way to ride, it is, contrary to one's immediate thinking, *not* beneficial from a conditioning standpoint. By doing this, a rider can do just as much damage as by forcing a horse into an overly rigid frame. If a horse always moves with his nose stuck out and his belly sagging, his poll will lose its pliability and he will unduly jar his limbs and joints.

Let's Talk Anatomy

The ring of muscles has a crucial effect on the horse's posture. The following discussion serves as the crux for this entire book and is something that you should keep at the forefront of your mind anytime you are working with horses.

In large measure, where a horse positions his head and neck while exercising determines whether he is using his ring of muscles. It is quite possible for a horse's neck to be in a relatively "good" position without his back being engaged properly. The primary factor here is whether the horse is *stretching* his neck forward into a good posture or merely holding it there in a static manner. Only the former action will make him a better day-to-day athlete.

Each vertebra in the horse's spine has little bony projections along its sides called "spinous processes." These projections are connected by a thick ligament called the supraspinous ligament,

which becomes the nuchal ligament from the withers forward. A sheet of elastic ligament tissue runs from both the nuchal ligament and the spinous processes in the withers to each neck vertebra; therefore, the neck acts as a lever with forward and upward traction on the rest of the spine.

When the horse stretches his neck forward to the rider's hands, as shown in the drawing below, his neck muscles and nuchal ligament create an upward traction on the spinous processes in the withers, which then pull the rest of the spine upward. When the spinous processes are lifted in a forward direction such as this, the horse's lower back and sacrum are automatically lifted, too.

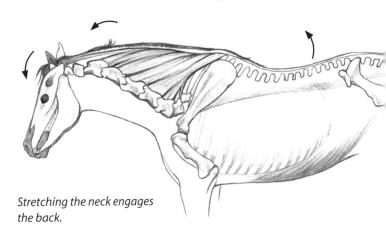

Stretching the neck engages the back.

spinous processes

nuchal ligament

supraspinous ligament

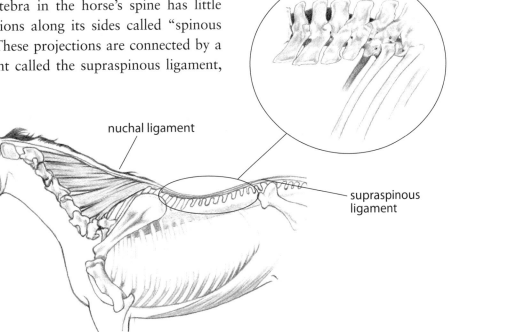

In the absence of a "bottom spine" along his belly, the horse's underside possesses a bundle of tendons that runs from forehand to hindquarters. When this bundle tightens, it pulls the sternum and pelvis toward each other. This happens as the back is lifted by the activity described above.

Is He Using His Ring?

When the horse uses his neck beneficially, no matter the discipline, it can be described as a "telescoping" gesture. It should look and feel underneath you that he is extending his neck outward, vertebra by vertebra, like a retractable telescope. Or, I like to think of it as the feeling the horse gives you when he arches his neck out and down to look at something on the ground near his front legs. Let's look at a few illustrations to show how the neck affects the rest of a horse's body.

When an unfit horse travels with "hollow" posture, his belly sags and pulls his back down.

Using the entire ring of muscles means that this horse is moving in a way that maximizes the benefits of conditioning and strengthening work.

This horse may look as though he is using his ring of muscles correctly, but he is carrying his neck too stiffly and his back is too hollow to allow him to benefit from the exercise he is doing.

Slight adjustments to posture ensure that the horse in the drawing to the left is using his ring of muscles. He may not be engaging them to the extreme that, say, a dressage horse does, but he is going about his exercise with a much more beneficial posture for enhanced conditioning and overall longevity and comfort.

The horse in the drawing above looks like it is in a decent frame, right? Look again. The neck looks at first like it is in a good shape, but if you look a little closer you will see that, in fact, it is not stretching forward. It is fixed in a forced or static manner. Recall our brief anatomical discussion above and check the illustration more closely.

Remember that when properly stretched, the neck muscles and ligaments will pull the rest of the horse's spine into a rounded shape, much like the ropes and rigging on a sailboat pulling the sail taut. If you look carefully at this horse's spine, you will see that it is, in fact, not round. In particular, look just behind the saddle. Instead of that area being flat or rounded, there is a small dip.

If the horse's neck were correctly engaging his ring of muscles, this dip would not be there. Because it is there, however, it guarantees that no matter what gymnastic exercises this horse performs, he will not make himself stronger or more supple. As long as his spine is *not* rounded upward, his pelvis cannot tuck and draw his back legs under his body. The short strides of his hind legs illustrate this.

Not asking for a particular posture can result in a horse that moves with a slack neck, flat back, and dragging legs, none of which will help him become more fit.

The above illustration shows a different version of a horse that is not using his back in a way that is beneficial for the rest of his body. This horse is certainly not in a forced posture. In fact, he's in no clear posture at all. This is a common frame for many horses who have weak or sensitive backs, such as Arabians and Thoroughbred-type breeds. It is also, unfortunately, a common posture assumed by many horses riding down the trail.

Although this posture is not forcing the horse into a frame, it is not good because the horse's ring of muscles is completely slack. Remember our pulley analogy. In this case, the pulleys and cables are loose, which means none of the horse's

musculoskeletal system has the proper amount of tone to work in a smooth, harmonious manner. Without the pulleys engaged, he just creates wear and tear on his body and stiffness in his limbs.

If you look closely, you will see that his abdominal muscles are disengaged and dropped toward the ground. You know from our earlier anatomical discussion that his lower back, therefore, is also sagging or hollow and his pelvis is tipped back behind him; his abdominal muscles are not toned enough to draw it forward and tuck it under him. This means his hind legs will continue to trail out behind rather than coming forward into balance under his mass.

How to Make Your Horse Stronger

Stiffness, asymmetries, and gait irregularities will not only persist but also worsen over time unless a horse is guided toward carrying himself in a better posture. It's not just the things that make your horse sweat and breathe heavily that strengthen him. Simple calisthenics can accomplish gymnastic results you may not have realized.

Arduous drilling of exercises is not the way to better fitness. Sometimes we believe that going to a gym and grunting really hard while straining to lift dumbbells is the way to gain strength. But in reality, the road to fitness does not require strain and grunting. Instead, basic exercise with good alignment, balance, and rhythmic breathing is all that's needed. Anyone who has ever practiced yoga or Pilates can attest to this.

For that reason, the exercises in this book are fairly simple. They do not seek to reinvent the wheel. They are proven methods of improving a horse's overall condition, soundness, and thereby his way of going. Horses are like us — a healthy, fit body leads to a happy mind and whatever we go about doing is then undertaken more energetically and with a higher level of performance. This, in turn, leads to more stamina, increased longevity of our limbs and joints, and freedom from pain or discomfort.

When you are undertaking any kind of riding with your horse, and *especially* when you are aiming to improve his performance level or condition him, you must ask yourself whether he is carrying himself in the correct posture. Riding him without proper engagement of his ring of muscles will only serve to deteriorate his gaits. On the other hand, if you go about his exercises with good use of his

KEY POINT

> Strength is acquired by simple movement only as long as the movement is correct. Remember: *Only perfect practice makes perfect.*

ring of muscles, you will improve his athleticism day after day. In my opinion, this is the only way to ride a horse.

Trust Your Horse to Use His Body Correctly

Although I advocate that riders be mindful of having their horses in the right posture to create healthy movement the majority of the time, there *are* instances where it is not only okay but necessary to allow the horse to get his job done however he pleases. This includes situations such as long-distance trail riding, where you must let the horse make his own choices about his frame because he knows better than you how to use himself to get the job done.

Or I should say, *if he is properly prepared, he will get the job done.* You should, therefore, do all of your preparation with insistence that he use his body healthily. Then, when a long-distance challenge comes along, give him the reins and let him use his well-prepared body the way he wants.

General Exercises for Strength

Some exercises place more demand on a horse's overall strength and physical power because they stress his muscles more than his cardiovascular system, coordination, and balance. These are the exercises that will be useful in improving your horse's strength and physical output. As you do these exercises, think about which ones — for your own horse — seem to demand more strength than, say, lung power or coordination.

Rein-back, for example, is enormously useful in training the equine athlete because it utilizes the horse's entire musculature. Crooked rein-backs reveal asymmetry in the horse's training and uneven use of the hind legs. Utilize rein-back (either done in hand or under saddle) at least 3 days a week. It is a very simple yet highly effective conditioning tool for the horse's postural muscles. Very few other exercises are so useful.

The proper execution of rein-back increases strength in the horse's hindquarters by asking his three major hind joints (sacrum, stifle, and hock) to flex and bear more weight. It stretches and strengthens the loins. The abdominal muscles must engage and draw the pubic bone forward, which tucks and lowers the horse's pelvis. Finally, walking backwards creates a rocking motion in the horse's sacrum, swinging it gently from side to side, which loosens the entire area in a way that other exercises do not.

When executed correctly, the rein-back should appear as though the horse is moving backwards with clear diagonal pairs (so that his left front leg and right rear leg, for example, step backward at the same moment). The horse's topline must continue to reach forward and round as the horse steps backward, as opposed to drawing his neck up and arching the back down.

WHAT'S THAT NOISE?

A couple of sounds that often crop up during ordinary riding sometimes worry or annoy riders. Many want to know why their horses are suddenly clicking, glugging, or popping! Let's take a quick look at these noises to put your mind at ease.

SHEATH SOUNDS
Several opinions swirl around about the noise that the sheath sometimes makes when a male horse is being exercised. Some people say the glugging or wind-sucking noise is due to a dirty sheath. Some will tell you it has something to do with conformation while others explain the noise only occurs when the horse is excited or nervous.

The real explanation for that noise is that the sheath is directly connected to the abdominal muscles. Stiffening or over tightening these muscles causes the sheath to change its normal position and make spasmodic movements, causing pockets of air to suck in and out. Over tightening can occur when a horse is excited or nervous, but also when he is fatigued from carrying a rider or stressed from maintaining a collected frame.

The noise is most often heard in horses with insufficient swing in their hind legs due to hollowing their backs. Common accompanying symptoms include: nervousness, lack of impulsion, or fatigue. The noise often disappears with loosening exercises that encourage a horse to relax his back and increase the reach of his hind legs.

SNAP, CRACKLE, POP
Almost every equestrian at some point has noticed a subtle clicking noise coming from the back end of her horse while riding or longeing or even leading. Some worry that it might be arthritis or indicate that the horse needs a joint supplement. The truth is that the noise isn't always coming from the joint and it's rarely reason for major concern.

Sometimes the noise *is* in the joint — hip, fetlock, knee — and it's similar to when human knees occasionally crack when we stand up. An air bubble becomes trapped in the joint capsule and when it squeezes out, it makes a cracking or popping noise.

More commonly, though, the noise is caused by tendons or ligaments, typically by joint ligaments. These thick ligaments are like elastic bands that hold joints together while allowing them to move. A clicking noise often happens when one of these ligaments flicks over the bone to a new position as the joint moves.

These noises can come and go, depending on a variety of factors such as the level of work the horse is doing and his conditioning. No pain or discomfort accompanies them, though there are a variety of ideas about how to possibly minimize the noises. One is to ensure that your horse receives sufficient minerals and a good source of fat (such as linseed meal, *not* corn oil) that help maintain pliability and moisture retention in soft tissues.

10. Rein-Back up a Hill 56

11. Rein-Back on a Curve 57

12. Turn on the Forehand in Motion 58

13. Exercise on a Slope 59

14. Riding a Drop 60

15. Canter to Walk Downhill (Gina Miles) 61

16. Gymnastic Jumping 62

17. Sets and Reps for Arena (Jennifer Bryant) 64

18. Double Longe (Mark Schuerman) 66

19. Arena Interval Training 68

STRENGTHENING EXERCISES

10. Rein-Back up a Hill

Backing your horse up a hill requires him to use his entire ring of muscles. It is perhaps the most useful strengthening *and* suppling tool to create a foundation for conditioning.

How Do I Do This?

1. Find a gentle uphill slope with hard ground. A driveway will suffice. Stand your horse with his hind end facing up the hill.

2. Ask your horse to lower his head, ideally to shoulder level, before beginning to back up.

3. Ask for as many steps backwards as possible, aiming for 10 at the minimum.

4. Each day, add four more steps.

5. If your horse becomes crooked or braces his neck/head upwards, stop the movement.

TIPS FOR SUCCESS: In the absence of a suitable hill, you can substitute a large pole for your horse to travel over backwards.

If your horse tends to put himself in a bad posture and raise his neck or drop his back, it is better to perform this exercise unmounted rather than under saddle. When executing the rein-back unmounted, use a gentle pressure on the halter or bridle to keep his neck low and use a crop aimed toward his chest to signal the rein-back.

The horse should maintain the rhythm of an ordinary walk — no faster, no slower. Do not ask for backward strides that are too long. Making the strides too long can throw the horse off balance and onto the forehand. Keep the movement rhythmic and balanced.

11. Rein-Back on a Curve

In addition to working the horse's core as in normal rein-back, this pattern increases symmetry in the horse by asking him to alternately push more off each individual hind leg.

How Do I Do This?

1. Designate a 10-meter circle using small cones or other markers.

2. Stand facing your horse, outside the cones.

3. Ask him to rein-back three straight strides to start.

4. Once you have that momentum, gently guide his shoulders slightly toward your left (away from you) and allow his hind end to swing to the right.

5. Continue walking him backwards around the 10-meter arc that you are now on.

6. If he loses the circle or gets stuck, you might need a long whip on the outside of his body to keep him on the circle.

7. Go halfway around the circle, then stop and praise him.

8. Finish the circle. Work your way up to being able to do the entire circle in one steady flow.

9. Repeat in the opposite direction.

TIPS FOR SUCCESS: Watch to see whether your horse steps the same length backwards with each hind leg. If not, he will show you which side of his body is uneven in its development. If your horse shows signs of worry or braces himself into a bad posture when on the curved line, go back to rein-back on a straight line to relax him and restore symmetry.

When you have mastered the above, try backing your horse up around a figure eight with two 10-meter circles so that you incorporate not only a curve in your rein-back but also a change of direction.

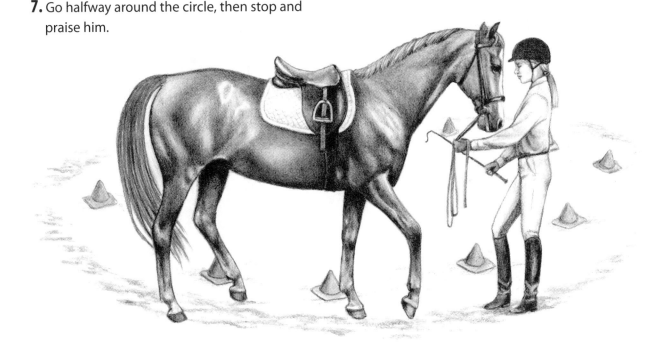

12. Turn on the Forehand in Motion

This basic exercise, like many, works because it both strengthens the horse and makes him more supple. As the side of the horse that is on the outside of the bend stretches accordingly, it assumes a certain amount of tone to stabilize the horse's trunk. The horse's ring of muscles is, therefore, engaged without the imbalances and asymmetries caused by forward movement. This exercise is equally valuable executed either in hand or under saddle.

A quick reminder about requirements for a correct turn on the forehand: the horse's front legs should remain in place and "mark time," that is, they should step up and down without moving forward. His hind legs should cross over, forming little X's with each stride. The exercise should be done in the same tempo and rhythm as if the horse were walking a straight line.

How Do I Do This?

1. Ride in a walk with light contact and the horse in a good posture.

2. Gently half halt with your seat and back to downshift.

3. As soon as the horse responds, bend him to the right and push his hindquarters away from your right leg.

4. Keep asking him to step his right hind leg in front of his left hind leg.

5. Keep a little bit of forward momentum in your turn so that the horse's front feet keep marching in half steps forward instead of coming to a complete stop.

6. After you have executed a 180-degree change of direction, ride straight forward and resume the normal energy of the walk.

7. Repeat in the opposite direction.

TIPS FOR SUCCESS: Ideally, the horse's hips should remain parallel to the ground. Otherwise, he is compromising his body and not benefiting from the movement. If you feel, or have someone tell you, that your horse is dropping a hip, adjust the size of your turn and amount of bend until you are able to remedy the problem.

13. Exercise on a Slope

Working a horse on sloped terrain encourages him to use his back in a way that improves looseness along his dorsal muscles and over his croup. On the descent portion of this pattern, the horse's abdominal muscles engage to balance him. On the ascent, his hip and back muscles engage. This exercise is highly useful in developing the horse's entire ring of core muscles and is indispensable for developing a strong back.

You will need to find a 20-meter-diameter circle area where the ground rises several feet on one side and slopes downward the same amount on the opposite side of the circle. The footing must be somewhat smooth and stable.

How Do I Do This?

1. Begin by longeing your horse at the walk to ensure he is managing his footwork on the uneven ground.

2. Once he is moving comfortably, pick up a trot around the circle. Keep the tempo slow.

3. Once your horse is trotting rhythmically around the circle, add a row of three or four ground poles to the bottom (downhill) side of the circle. They should be spaced appropriately for your horse to take only one trot stride between each one. The poles will encourage propulsion and a rhythmic stride.

4. Once your horse is negotiating the ground poles comfortably, add a small jump or crossrail at the uppermost portion of the top (uphill) side of the circle. This way, the horse finishes his ascent with propulsion before rebalancing for the downhill section.

TIP FOR SUCCESS: Keep the speed slow and easy enough for your horse to maintain the same rhythm all the way around the circle, rather than changing his rhythm from the uphill to the downhill portion.

14. Riding a Drop

This is strictly a strength-training exercise that builds propulsion in the horse's hindquarters. It builds strength by first asking the hindquarter to flex, or coil, and then propel the rest of his mass into the air. It's a brief but more intense use of the muscles engaged in riding up hills.

If you do not have a drop constructed at your barn, you can easily make one. You can construct one in a small area utilizing already-sloped ground, railroad ties, ditches, or whatever is handy. All that matters it that the horse has roughly a 2- to 3-foot (0.5–1 m) drop to jump into with stable ground on the opposite side to jump onto.

How Do I Do This?

1. Approach the drop straight on at the walk, making sure that your horse is facing it straight and not crooked.

2. Just at the edge of the drop down, ask him to stop. Stand quietly for a few seconds to focus his attention on the drop.

3. From a standstill, ask him to step down into the drop. Keep your momentum going forward from this point, but not rushing. You want all four of his feet to step down in a balanced manner.

4. As soon as you are in the drop, urge him on with more energy. Ideally, he will jump his way out of the hole, rather than scrambling out.

5. Repeat three times.

TIP FOR SUCCESS: You may need to urge him more energetically and with a slightly forward seat if he does not respond by jumping out.

15. Canter to Walk Downhill

Contributed by Gina Miles, 2008 Silver Medalist in the Olympics, Pan American Games, and World Equestrian Games

This strenuous exercise strengthens the horse in a number of ways. Primarily, it improves his balance and way of carrying himself because of the weight transfer to his hindquarters that needs to happen for him to execute it successfully. In addition, when there is that transfer of weight, the horse tucks his hindquarters underneath his body mass (think of a cat crouching), which strengthens the muscles of his lower back and entire hind end. You can modify the exercise to a trot–halt format going downhill.

For riders who work primarily in an arena setting, such as adult amateur dressage riders or breed-show participants, cantering downhill can seem like a big, fast, scary deal. Bear in mind, however, that it's actually *not* a big deal for most horses. They canter downhill in nature — with darn good balance — all the time and, in many ways, it's more comfortable for them than trotting downhill. This exercise might stretch your comfort zone, but every good conditioning program does that now and then!

How Do I Do This?

1. Warm up for 10 minutes with Cantering on Uneven Terrain (page 113), finishing at the top of the slope.

2. Proceed in a slow canter straight down a gentle grade.

3. Pick a midpoint on the downhill slope and transition into a walk.

4. Keep your horse straight in the transition; do not allow him to get crooked.

5. Walk the remainder of the slope.

6. Trot or canter to the top of the hill.

7. This time, divide the hill in thirds (if it is long enough) and at each third, transition from canter to walk. Then walk four strides and canter again to the next transition point.

8. Build up to being able to execute 10 of these transitions on each canter lead.

TIP FOR SUCCESS: If you are not able to get a reasonably slow canter with your horse (if, perhaps, he is green, stiff, or unbalanced), this exercise will be exceptionally difficult. In this instance, take a few lessons from your instructor focusing specifically on having your horse respond well to a half halt from your seat to slow down and balance himself in the arena first.

16. Gymnastic Jumping

The merits of jumping are well-known. Hopping over small jumps encourages flexion of the hindquarters, rounding of the back, and telescoping outward of the neck. In jumping, the horse's ligaments, bones, and tendons are strengthened in a way that cannot be achieved by flat work alone. Jumping is, however, most useful in terms of conditioning when enough repetitions are performed for these reflexes to occur frequently in one session.

This exercise requires the use of a simple grid of jumps as shown in the diagram. Place three trot poles on the ground approximately one trot stride apart. Then set up a cross-rail at a height of approximately 1 to 2 feet (0.3–0.6 m) spaced about 8 feet (2.5 m) away from the last trot pole.

How Do I Do This?

1. Develop an active working trot.

2. Trot *straight* over the *middle* of the three trotting poles.

3. After crossing the last one, come into a half-seat or two-point position.

4. Go forward over the cross-rail.

5. Give your horse a short rest by trotting once around the edge of the entire arena.

6. Repeat for a total of 20 minutes, including the "rest" periods where you trot around the edge of the entire arena.

TIPS FOR SUCCESS: If your horse is not "jumping" but rather trotting over the cross-rail, you may need to either raise it slightly or encourage him to approach it with more energy.

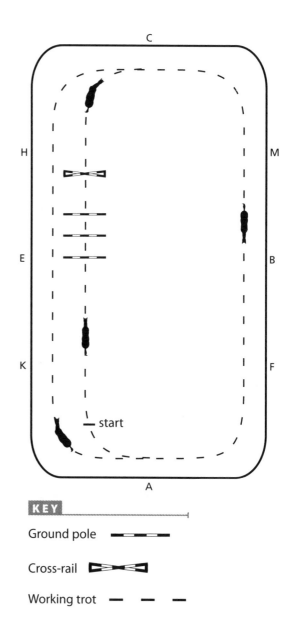

KEY

Ground pole

Cross-rail

Working trot

VARIATION

This exercise asks more of the horse because the canter stride and additional jump require more coiling of his loins and use of his haunches. You will use the same setup as for the previous exercise, with the addition of another cross-rail jump about 18 feet (5.5 m) from the first one.

How Do I Do This?

1. Trot straight over the three ground poles and over the first cross-rail.

2. Immediately canter one stride straight ahead to the second cross-rail.

3. If you have trouble getting your horse into the canter before the second jump, space yourself more until your horse understands.

4. Rest him at the trot for 2 minutes around the edge of the arena before repeating.

TIPS FOR SUCCESS: Keep your balance in the saddle so that your horse can find his. Sit with a tall but light seat. Maintain a steady unhurried rhythm and hold a *straight* line.

KEY	
Ground pole	▭▬▭
Cross-rail	▷◁
Working trot	— — —
Canter	– – –° – – –°

17. Sets and Reps for Arena

Contributed by **Jennifer Bryant,** Author of *The USDF Guide to Dressage*

By interspersing higher-intensity periods of schooling during your arena workout with "rest" sets, you gain more benefit overall. Your horse's mind and body have a chance to recover during the rest sets and he is able to make a greater physical output — and derive more conditioning benefit — during the next work set.

Even when riding in the arena, think of the session in terms of "sets and reps," as in a strength-training workout. Follow each short period of higher-intensity work with a break of equal length. Walk on a loose rein, or allow him to stretch forward and down over his topline. This is a challenging exercise suitable for more advanced riders and horses.

How Do I Do This?

- Perform *one* of the work sets for 5 minutes.
- Allow your horse to rest for 5 minutes. Depending on your horse's fitness and energy level, "rest" might mean stretching on a long rein at the walk or trotting easily in a stretched outline.
- Work for 4 minutes and rest for 4 minutes.
- Work for 3 minutes and rest for 3 minutes.
- Work for 2 minutes, final rest, and cooldown.

TIPS FOR SUCCESS: Many times, it is the rider — rather than the horse — who needs to maintain the "oomph" during the high-intensity work sets. Really *go for it* because a well-deserved rest is waiting for you!

If anything, you want to push yourself and your horse for a little more energy, good form, balance, etc., during each working period. The final 2-minute set should be almost perfect and really exerting.

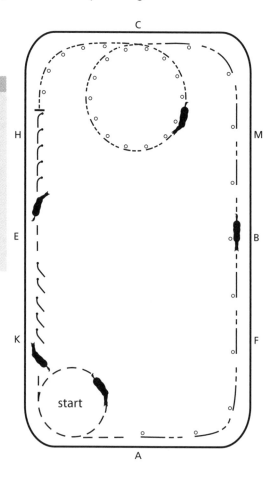

WORK SET A

1. Execute working or collected trot on a 10-meter circle twice.

2. Ride halfway down the long side in haunches-in, then change to shoulder-in for remaining half of long side.

3. At the end, straighten your horse and pick up a working or collected canter. Canter twice around an approximately 15-meter circle and go down the long side in extended canter.

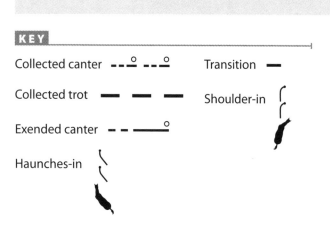

KEY

Collected canter

Collected trot

Exended canter

Haunches-in

Transition

Shoulder-in

1. In active working trot, go straight over a row of five raised ground poles.

2. Pick up a canter and ride a shallow loop down the long side and come back to the trot.

3. Turn down the centerline and leg-yield to the rail.

4. Canter halfway around the arena again.

5. Halt and rein-back eight steps.

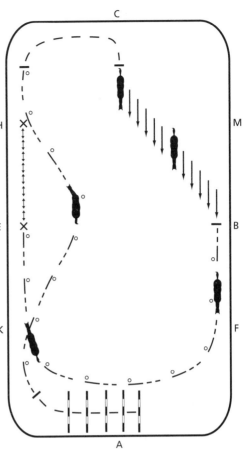

KEY

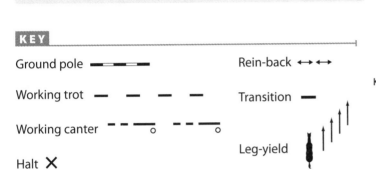

Ground pole

Working trot

Working canter

Halt ✕

Rein-back ↔ ↔

Transition ▬

Leg-yield

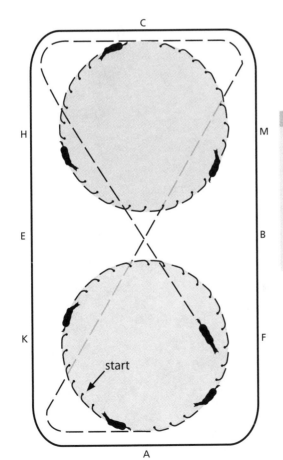

1. Perform shoulder-in in working or collected trot on an approximately 20-meter circle.

2. Proceed across the diagonal in extended trot.

3. Ride 20-meter circle in shoulder-in in the new direction and then across the diagonal again in extended trot.

KEY

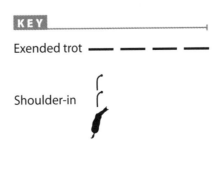

Exended trot

Shoulder-in

18. Double Longe

Contributed by Mark Schuerman, Multinational Champion for Arabians and Half-Arabians in Sport Horse Under Saddle, Show Hack, and Dressage Disciplines

This is a focused way of exercising your horse's topline when you are short on time or not able to ride for some reason. Because of how it "shapes" the horse, double longeing is preferable from a conditioning standpoint to regular longeing with a single line.

Your horse must accept the feeling of a rope touching his back legs for this exercise. Before you begin, outfit him with a proper surcingle (one with multiple rings down both sides) and basic snaffle bridle.

How Do I Do This?

1. Begin by lining up your horse to make a large circle to the left, then halt him and make him stand still.

2. Attach the inside line as shown in A. Keep a hand on this line for safety while attaching your outside line.

3. Attach the outside line as shown in B and run it behind his buttocks, just above his hock.

4. Holding the inside in your left hand and the outside line plus a long whip in your right, step back toward the middle of the circle. Your horse must stand quietly as you do this.

5. Organize your lines and send your horse forward into a brisk trot.

6. Keep your horse trotting vigorously the whole time so that he rounds his topline into the contact with the ground-driving lines.

7. Do 10 minutes in each direction. When you change directions, don't forget to switch the hookup of your lines.

A

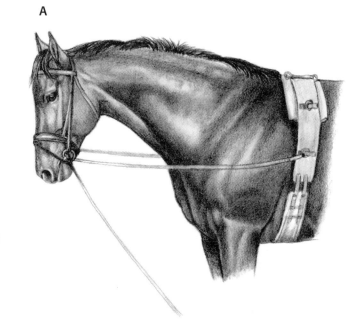

B

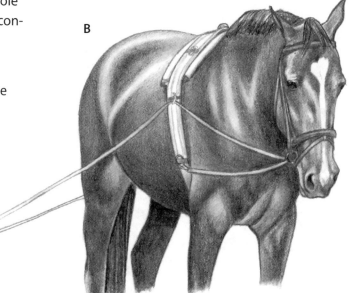

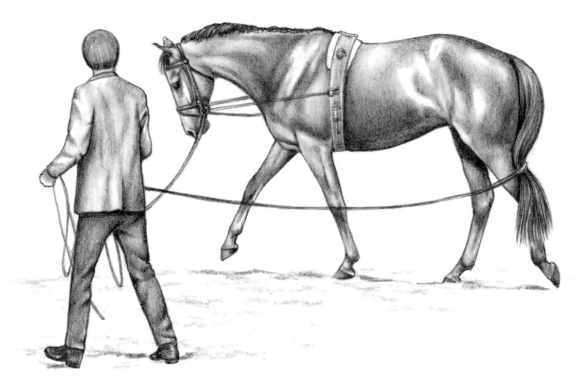

Keep a light feel in both reins and be sure the outside line does not drop below the horse's hock.

EQUIPMENT TIP: Having the right equipment makes a big difference in this exercise. Insufficient lines or a surcingle without the proper rigging will make your life very difficult. Commercial longe lines are often too lightweight and hard to handle. I prefer to make my own ground-driving lines from climbing rope by attaching a heavy-duty snap to about 30 feet (9 m) of rope. Sailing rope also has a nice weight.

TIP FOR SUCCESS: Double longeing is most suitable for trotting work and not so much the walk or canter because, in those gaits, it can restrict the oscillating neck.

19. Arena Interval Training

An interval is a short burst of speed that increases the heart rate, followed by a brief rest period during which the horse's heart rate is kept at working level. Interval training will help improve or maintain your horse's overall cardiovascular fitness. If you want to increase, rather than maintain, fitness over time, gradually add a second work set after the long walk break.

How Do I Do This?

1. Walk your horse briskly on a long rein for 5 to 10 minutes to warm up.

2. Canter at a moderate pace around the track of your arena for 2 full minutes.

3. Transition down and do a working trot for 2 minutes. This is your "rest" period.

4. Canter in the opposite direction for 2 minutes.

5. Repeat the canter-trot-canter sequence four times for a total of 24 minutes.

6. After the fourth set, bring your horse down to a walk. Allow him to walk at ease for a full 10 minutes until breathing and heart rate return to a resting rate.

TIPS FOR SUCCESS: Follow the steps precisely and be consistent. Try to perform a cardiovascular workout of this type at least once weekly.

Remember to cool down. Allow nearly 20 minutes of hacking around or walking for the horse to recover from this workout.

Be aware of your footing. Different riding surfaces can tax your horse more than you realize. Loose, sandy arenas, for example, will strain your horse far more than firmer ones. You may need to modify the outlined intervals depending on your arena.

WARMING UP AND COOLING DOWN

Unfortunately, the warm-up and cool-down are often overlooked or are aimless portions of a workout. I encourage you to give thought each day to whether your warm-up routine readies the horse's body for the work ahead or just moves him around without specific focus. A focused warm-up determines, in large measure, how much your horse will gain from the workout.

Just because your horse is moving around on the end of a longe line, meandering down the trail, or going through his paces under saddle at the beginning of a session does not automatically ensure that he is warming up properly. What is needed is, first, a loosening-up phase and, second, a period with enough vigorous activity to increase blood flow and oxygen.

The overall goal of warming up is to increase oxygen delivery to the horse's musculature to prevent the early accumulation of lactic acid during the workout. (See page 20 for more on lactic acid.) In addition to causing fatigue, lactic-acid buildup also prohibits the horse from benefiting from the workout; the muscles are not nourished and elastic enough to gain in strength from exercise

so, instead, they accumulate waste products. To counter this, you want to stimulate enough oxygen and blood circulation to the horse's muscles in the beginning to nourish them and keep them functioning at 100 percent throughout the workout as well as limit the buildup of waste products that cause post-workout soreness.

KEY POINT

How well the body is readied for its exercise directly correlates to how much benefit it receives from workouts. The purpose of warming up is to bring the horse's muscles to a state of readiness for further work.

The Difference between Loosening Up and Warming Up

Some people believe that riding around on long reins at a walk at the beginning of a session serves as a sufficient warm-up. Although a vital part of the everyday ride, this activity does not adequately increase oxygen and blood flow to the horse's muscles. It's important, therefore, to differentiate the purpose of this phase from the actual warm-up phase. When you first mount up, you *should* spend a few moments allowing your horse to walk around on a long rein, especially if he lives in confined quarters much of the day. This gentle activity allows his joints to regain mobility. As the fluids begin moving and lubricating, the movement gradually brings his respiration rate up and gives his muscles time to limber up.

This phase also allows the horse to adjust mentally to the workout ahead. It gives him time to settle and relax, which will make his body more adept for the task at hand. For some horses, this phase needs to last only 3 minutes or so. For older horses, it may require up to 10 minutes. But, generally, two laps around the arena should suffice for most horses.

The Warm-up Phase

Following the initial phase of loosening up, you can begin to increase the intensity of your exercise, allowing the muscles to gradually increase their working temperature, which makes them more pliable. Once you begin the warm-up phase, keep it *active* because the point is to increase blood flow to the skeletal muscles.

This does not happen at a wandering pace, or if you trot actively for a minute, stop to chat with someone outside the arena, and then start trotting again, and so on. Once you begin moving the horse actively forward, keep going! A few points to bear in mind:

- Maintain contact with the horse's mouth and ask that he carry himself with good posture.
- Keep any ridden figures/patterns very simple at this stage, utilizing mostly straight lines, changes of direction, and large circles.
- Avoid tight turns, serpentines, and similar movements.
- Use the rising trot, never a sitting trot, to keep the horse's back as loose and unrestrained as possible.

- When cantering, sit in a light seat, slightly inclined forward from your hips, so that you do not drive your seat bones down into the horse's back muscles before they are fully warmed up and engaged.

There is no rule about whether trot or canter suits your warm-up best. Every horse is different. Some are more balanced in the canter and prefer it; therefore, it is perfectly acceptable to use it for your warm-up. Others, however, move and carry themselves better in the trot, which would be more suitable for their warm-ups.

This phase of actively riding the horse forward to stimulate blood flow and pliability of his muscles should last from 5 to 10 minutes. From that point on, the horse's tendons and ligaments will be warm enough that you can begin to add suppling exercises into your riding. For the following 5 or 10 minutes you can continue riding actively but begin to progressively add more gymnastic demands such as smaller circles, serpentines, leg-yield, and other lateral movements if your horse knows them.

Be Strategic

As your warm-up continues, you want to ride increasingly more strenuous gymnastic exercises and patterns. For example, you'll want to go from riding very large circles in the beginning to riding 10-meter voltes, or from riding shallow loops and turns to three-loop serpentines. After you have been riding your horse for 15 or 20 minutes, this progressive warm-up should blend seamlessly into your conditioning session for the day or into your normal schooling routine of collection and transitions between gaits, patterns, lateral movements, and so on. If you are jumping, you can now tackle higher fences, having ridden over only low ones at the end of your warm-up phase. If you are on the trail, you can transition from gradual gradients to more demanding terrain.

Allowing your horse to loosen up before you begin your formal warm-up is crucial for his preparation mentally as well as physically.

Once you begin your warm-up, stay focused on bringing your horse into his exercise or training routine. Don't be aimless!

The Critical Cooldown

Properly cooling down is as important as properly warming up, particularly in any extreme weather — either chilly and windy or excessive heat and humidity even after a short ride. Going back to stand in a stall after a workout is the worst thing for your horse. Do not assume, however, that if he lives in a paddock or pasture he will move around in the right way to cool himself down.

Toward the end of your riding session, begin to gradually lessen the intensity of your workout and resume a basic easy trot forward for a few minutes. This means no more gymnastic patterns or interval training work or steep gradients. Then, you will want to walk your horse either under saddle or in hand for 10 to 15 minutes, even if he seems to be breathing normally and not sweating any longer.

Why walk even if his body temperature feels cool to the touch? Because the horse's muscles act as pumps that move waste material out of his muscular system and back to his heart, where it can be recirculated and flushed from his tissues. When a horse stands around after a riding session, circulation slows and wastes pool in the muscles, creating soreness and stiffness and filling the horse's joints. A brisk walk after a riding session will go far in leaving the horse feeling well for his next ride.

KEY POINT The practice of walking the first mile out and the first mile back on a trail ride provides the perfect warm-up and cooldown. A short trail ride after a workout session can be a great way to cool out your horse and reward him (and yourself) for a job well done.

If your horse is excessively hot or sweaty after an exercise session, or the weather is quite warm, you will want to hose him off to help with the cooling process. This does *not* mean that splashing cold water over his entire body will do the trick. The idea is to use tepid water only in the most vascular areas (belly, bottom of the neck, legs) that are pumping and circulating blood to cool the rest of the body.

Cold water will cause his blood vessels to restrict in response to the sharp difference in temperature, which is counterproductive. Expanded vessels dispel heat more quickly and efficiently.

Because the horse's lower legs are constructed entirely of tendons with no muscles below his knees, you also want to eliminate any heat in his tendons. Otherwise, persistent heat or inflammation can accumulate day to day in those crucial tendons and lead to an unexpected breakdown.

Cooling down takes time as the horse's large body mass requires a gradual return to its resting state. Throwing water at your horse for 5 minutes and then putting him back in his stall will not achieve the right aim.

Within 5 minutes, his outward muscles may feel cool to the touch, but his tendons, ligaments, and respiratory structures will most likely still be experiencing a gradual decrease in circulation and adapting again to a resting state. Don't forget about the parts you cannot see. Give them time to *thoroughly* cool out.

The dark areas show where you should apply tepid (not cold) water to most effectively cool down an overheated horse.

20. Tail Pull 74

21. Tail Rotations 75

22. Lateral Cervical Flexion (Jim Masterson). 76

23. Shoulder Release Down and Back (Jim Masterson) 78

24. Shoulder Release Down and Forward (Jim Masterson) 80

25. Loosening the Back 82

26. Warm-up 1 — The Oval 83

27. Warm-up 2 — Simple Trot Pattern 84

28. Shoulder-In to Shallow Serpentine (Betsy Steiner) 85

29. Canter on the Honor System (Jessica Jahiel) 86

20. Tail Pull

The tail, which ties into the spinal column, consists of numerous joints, between 11 and 15 depending on a horse's breed and conformation. Stretching it affects the horse's entire back.

How Do I Do This?

1. Standing about an arm's length directly behind your horse's buttocks, grasp his tail above the end of the tailbone.

2. With your feet firmly planted, gently pull the tail straight out from the horse's back.

3. Hold for 20 seconds, maintaining a consistent amount of traction.

4. Release very slowly so that the horse's back muscles can ease out of the stretch.

5. Work up to holding this stretch for 2 minutes.

TIPS FOR SUCCESS: You can incorporate tail traction into your grooming routine. Aim to do it before and after each ride. In chilly weather, however, do it only after riding.

If your horse shifts from side to side, clamps his tail, or stamps his feet when you try this stretch, his spinal vertebrae may be out of alignment. You should consult an equine chiropractor.

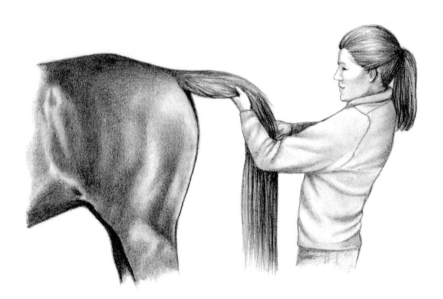

21. Tail Rotations

This stretch has a stretching effect similar to the Tail Pull with the additional benefit of loosening the sides of the horse's back. It is worth taking the time to have your horse accept this stretch. Not only will he learn to love it but also it loosens his back muscles wonderfully!

How Do I Do This?

1. Stand close behind or slightly off to the side of your horse, behind his hip on one side.

2. Hold the dock of his tail (about 4 inches [10 cm] from the top of his tail) with both hands and lift gently straight up.

3. Lift the tail upward 2 to 4 inches (5–10 cm) away from the ground.

4. Make small circular motions with the tail, circling in each direction three to five rotations.

5. Be sure your circles are evenly sized in both directions of rotations. If not, it might be an indication of stiffness or tightness in the horse's back.

6. Move slowly in this stretch so the horse does not clamp his tail.

TIP FOR SUCCESS: Some horses are initially resistant to having their tails lifted and will clamp them between their buttocks. You can get your horse to relax by gently rubbing the hairless underside at the dock. Once he relaxes, move into the circling motion.

22. Lateral Cervical Flexion

Contributed by Jim Masterson, Former Equine Massage Therapist for the United States Equestrian Team

This exercise releases tension in the poll and neck to improve their abilities to flex both laterally and vertically. As a general rule, when tension in the poll is released, the entire body relaxes. Once your horse understands and experiences the release of tension, this simple exercise will flow quicker each day. It is incredibly valuable in your warm-up.

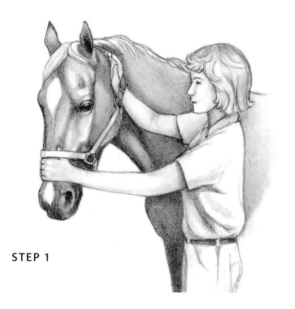

STEP 1

How Do I Do This?

1. Standing beside your horse next to his left shoulder, place your left hand gently on the nose or noseband and your right hand or fingertips below and behind the atlas (the first cervical vertebra, located about 4 inches [10 cm] below and behind the ear).

2. Gently flex the nose toward you with your left hand and apply very gentle pressure toward the opposite ear with your right hand. You are asking (not forcing) the horse to relax the atlas. Watch for the eye to soften, feeling for a release of tension in the atlas and poll. Signs of release of tension are repeated blinking, yawning, licking and chewing, snorting, sneezing, and "shaking it loose." Look for these signs as you work.

3. Slightly relax both hands and then move your right hand 2 or 3 inches (5–7.5 cm) down the vertebrae of the neck, keeping your left hand on the nose.

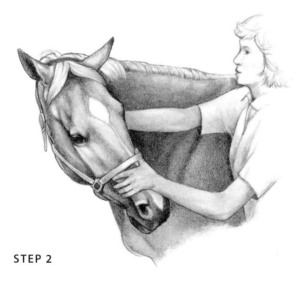

STEP 2

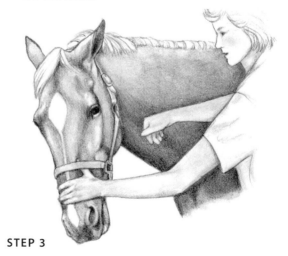

STEP 3

4. Gently flex his head toward you again with the left hand, pushing gently away with the right hand. Bring the nose a little farther back toward the shoulder, stepping back as you go.

5. Relax both hands again and move the right hand farther down the vertebrae of the neck.

6. Bring the horse's nose farther back toward the shoulder each time until you have brought the head all the way back to the shoulder and your hand all the way down to the lower vertebrae of the neck. As the horse relaxes, gently rock the head and neck with both hands as you go.

7. Step back and allow the horse to release. Duplicate the exercise on the opposite side.

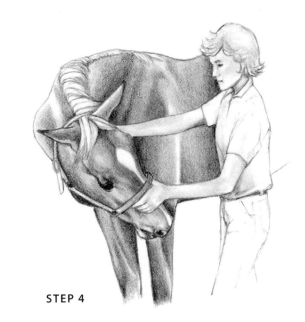

STEP 4

STEP 7

TIPS FOR SUCCESS: Generally, it is best to start on the left side of the horse; however, if your horse shows more resistance bending to one side, start on the opposite side.

If the horse fidgets or fusses at any time during the process, do not take your hands off, but soften and release the pressure, then immediately ask again. Fidgeting is often a sign that the horse is about to release. When you soften, it gives him a chance to do so.

23. Shoulder Release Down and Back

Contributed by Jim Masterson, Former Equine Massage Therapist for the United States Equestrian Team

Even with correct training and conditioning, horses hold a lot of tension at the base of their necks, just as humans do. Alleviating that tension improves overall range of motion. You will feel a difference! The purpose of this exercise is to release tension in the junction of neck/shoulder/withers and to improve forelimb extension and mobility in the front end. This is not a muscle stretch; you are assisting the horse to *release* tension, not just pulling on the limb.

How Do I Do This?

1. Position yourself at the horse's left shoulder, facing forward.

2. Lift the foot and place your right hand on the inside of the fetlock and your left hand under the horse's knee. Make sure your right hand is on or above the fetlock, not on the hoof.

3. Hold the leg in this position, allowing the muscles of the shoulder to relax. When you feel the leg and shoulder relax or drop slightly, move on to the next step. The idea is for the horse to relax the leg in your hands until he sets it down and back. Wiggling or rotating the foot and leg may help him to relax. If there is a lot of tension in the shoulder he may have trouble relaxing in this position. If so, move on to the next step right away. Do not pull on the leg.

STEP 2

TIPS FOR SUCCESS: *Be sure to straighten his leg and allow him to put his foot down!* If you hold his foot up and he can't put it down, he will pull back up or fall down on his knee (not good). This is why your right hand has to be above the pastern.

Usually the horse will relax the leg down to a certain point and then pull up again. Do not pull on his leg at this point, but hold it up until he relaxes again, then ask him to set it down. We want him to relax through this point of restriction.

4. When he is relaxed, lower his foot with your right hand, straighten his leg with your left hand, and ask him to put his foot down and back until it is flat on the ground. Feel for his shoulder blade (scapula) to drop slightly as he does this. Do not ask him to step back too far.

5. Allow the horse to release. The horse may stay in this position as long as he wants or he may go back to a normal stance.

6. Duplicate the exercise on the opposite side.

STEP 4

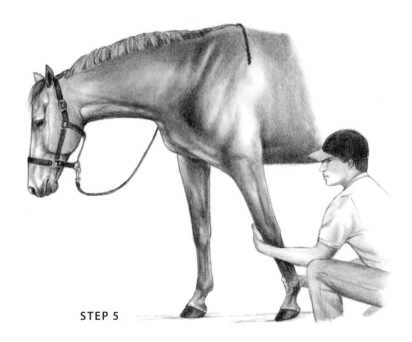

STEP 5

24. Shoulder Release Down and Forward

Contributed by **Jim Masterson,** Former Equine Massage Therapist for the United States Equestrian Team

The purpose of this exercise is to release tension in the neck/shoulder/withers junction to improve forelimb extension and mobility in the front end. This is not a muscle stretch. The idea is for the horse to relax the leg in your hands until he puts it down and slightly forward. Do not pull on the leg.

How Do I Do This?

1. Position yourself at the horse's left shoulder, facing toward the hind end.

2. Lift the foot with your hand under the fetlock as if you were going to clean the hoof.

3. Step backward bringing the foot with you, with one hand under the fetlock and the other under the bulb of the heel, so that the leg is extending slightly forward.

4. With the leg slightly forward, support the leg either with the fingers of both hands under the toe or under the bulb of the heel. *Important: If the horse falls forward into your hand, put the foot down. Do not keep pulling forward.*

5. When he is relaxed, slide your right hand under the bulb of the heel and lower his foot to the ground, keeping your left hand on his shoulder. Feel for his shoulder blade (scapula) to drop slightly as he does this. Do not pull his leg out too far.

STEP 4

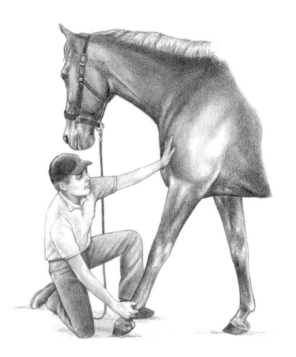

STEP 5

6. Step back and allow the horse to release. As he releases his leg down and forward, pick a spot on the ground close to the horse for him to put his foot. Do not continue to hold the foot out because he could fall forward or hyperextend the leg — not good!

7. Repeat this exercise on the opposite side.

TIP FOR SUCCESS: Allow the horse to stay in position as long as he wants or to return to a normal stance. Signs of releasing tension are repeated blinking, yawning, licking and chewing, snorting, sneezing, and "shaking it loose." Look for these signs as you work.

STEP 6

25. Loosening the Back

I learned this exercise from watching video clips of dressage masters when I was a child — Klimke, von Neindorff, Lindgren. One thing they all seemed to do before any formal workout was to saddle their horses and walk them repeatedly over a line of ground poles on a loose rein. The gentle increased articulation of the horse's hind legs as he moves over the poles, along with the stretching forward motion of his neck and greater scapula rotation that accompanies the exercise, loosen his back and spine in a natural and unforced way. In addition, the entirely loose rein contact in this exercise provides a few moments of complete mental relaxation.

How Do I Do This?

1. Set up five ground poles outside your arena on flat ground. (If possible, leave them set up permanently.) They should be spaced approximately 3.5 feet (1.07 m) apart from one another so that your horse can walk comfortably over them without taking a stride *between* any of them.

2. Before heading into the arena for your work-out, ride over the poles.

3. Continue straight back and forth over them until you feel your horse's stride change; that is, he begins to keep a steady cadence over the poles and is reaching nicely with a long stride over the poles, beginning to round up his back under your seat, and stretching his neck toward the ground.

4. On some days, it may require several trips over the poles (up to 10 or more) until you notice a change; on other days, your horse may loosen up after crossing the poles only twice.

5. After you feel your horse's muscles becoming looser, establish your contact and head to the arena for your workout.

TIPS FOR SUCCESS: Take the time in this simple warm-up exercise to work on yourself. This is a perfect opportunity to work on your seat — sitting deeply, *following* the movement, keeping your eyes *up*, and stretching your legs down from your hip.

Remember to keep your horse *straight* over the middle of the poles.

Note any changes in the way he feels from day to day. Does he bump into the poles when you start? Is he distracted? Does his back seem sore and unwilling to round up? Is he resisting your aids to be straight?

26. Warm-up 1 — The Oval

Remember that the aim of warming up after the initial walking/loosening phase is to increase blood and oxygen flow to really get the muscles working and moving. The following exercise is excellent for building up the horse's energy and progressively increasing his cardiovascular response to the day's workout ahead.

How Do I Do This?

1. Visualize a giant oval around the edge of your arena.

2. On the long sides of your oval, ride a big ground-covering trot with lots of energy.

3. As you come to the rounded ends on the top and bottom of your oval, markedly downshift to a slower trot.

4. As you come out of the rounded ends, immediately step on the gas and ask your horse to surge forward in a big, bold trot down the long side of the arena again.

5. Downshift again coming into the top/bottom of your oval. Continue this sequence for several minutes, practicing in both directions.

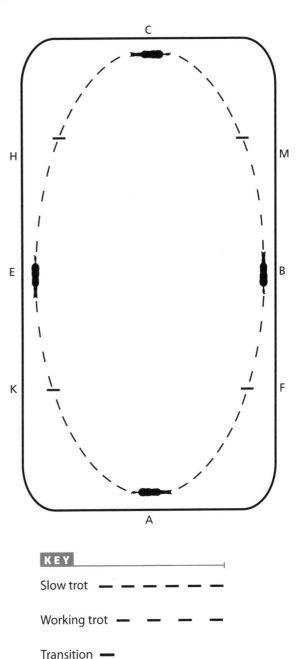

KEY

Slow trot — — — — — —

Working trot — — — — —

Transition —

27. Warm-up 2 — Simple Trot Pattern

This exercise is a variation of the previous one with the added benefit of using a curved line/circle to warm up the joints by asking the horse to gently bend his spine laterally.

How Do I Do This?

1. Begin in an energetic working trot to the right.

2. Ride once around the edge of the arena, maintaining a steady rhythm.

3. At A, ride one 20-meter circle.

4. As soon as you leave the circle and are on a straight line again, ask your horse to increase his trot tempo to cover as much ground as possible.

5. At the opposite end of the arena, resume your steady working trot tempo. When you come around to A again, ride another 20-meter circle and repeat step 4.

6. Repeat this a few times and then execute the same pattern in the canter.

7. Repeat in the opposite direction.

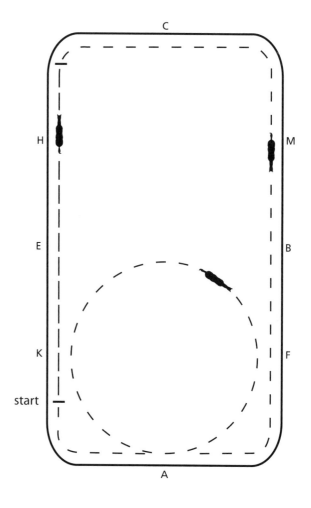

KEY

Working trot — — —

Lengthened trot —— ——

28. Shoulder-In to Shallow Serpentine

Contributed by **Betsy Steiner**, Former Member of the United States Dressage Team

This exercise builds the horse's strength by having him flex the joints of his hindquarters and is suitable for any horse that has learned how to bend and move off the leg. The pattern helps keep him supple and loose while building strength, without enabling him to brace or get tense. If you do not have dressage markers in your arena, set up any other kind of visual targets so you can ensure proper geometry.

How Do I Do This?

1. In an active trot, ride shoulder-in for the first third of your arena's long side (K–V).

2. "Peel" off the rail and ride to X.

3. At X, change your horse's bend to the left and ride back to the rail at H.

4. Once you return to the rail at H, ride a 10-meter circle to the right.

5. Proceed the rest of the way around the arena to repeat exercise again at K.

TIPS FOR SUCCESS: Keep a consistent rhythm throughout all the pieces of this short pattern. Maintain an energetic trot to sustain the right muscle output to build strength. Work in both directions.

VARIATION

Shoulder-In to a Diagonal in the Trot

Follow the above pattern through step 3, except once you peel off the rail, extend your horse's trot strides all the way across the arena to M. When you get to the rail at M, slow down a bit and reorganize his working trot.

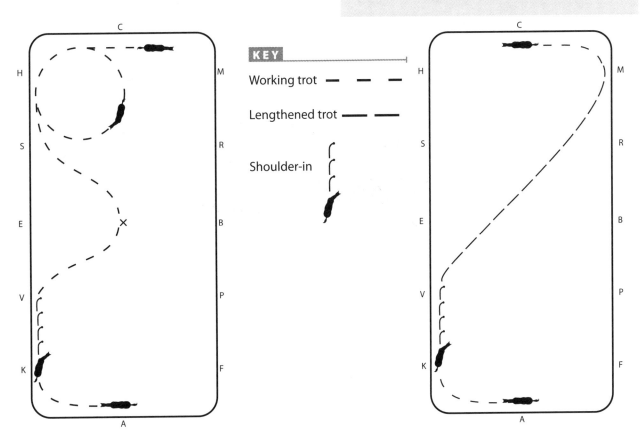

KEY

Working trot — — — —

Lengthened trot —— ——

Shoulder-in

29. Canter on the Honor System

Contributed by Dr. Jessica Jahiel, Internationally recognized author, trainer, and instructor

For the horse, this exercise promotes muscular development from hindquarters to poll, as well as mental trust and relaxation, increased trust in his own balance, and increased trust in his rider. It encourages the rider to follow the horse with seat and hands, and to use posture and balance — not the reins! — to effect changes.

The rider's focus is on creating impulsion and allowing the horse to express that impulsion. The rider cannot hold the horse's head and neck in a particular position to create or maintain a specific silhouette; thus we eliminate a common cause of physical and mental tension that can negate the body- and mind-building effects of many canter exercises.

How Do I Do This?

1. Warm up thoroughly at the walk, and perhaps also (depending on your horse's fitness and flexibility) at the trot.

2. When warmed up, go into a light half-seat, lengthen your reins until they are *loose* rather than *long*, and allow/encourage your horse to canter on a large circle (at least 20 meters).

3. Continue cantering for at least 5 minutes and possibly much longer, depending on your horse's level of fitness.

TIPS FOR SUCCESS: Hunter riders will recognize this as "cantering on the buckle"; dressage riders as "going long, low, and engaged." Endurance riders may not have a name for it, but they frequently use it when conditioning their horses. The essence is the same: to continue cantering until, and after, the horse is relaxed.

This exercise is pleasant for the horse but can be challenging for the rider. There is no use of reins and no sitting deep in the saddle — your contact and communication with the horse come from your legs, weight and balance, breathing, and voice.

CHAPTER

6

THE MIGHTY NECK

So FAR, WE'VE DISCUSSED THE NECESSITY of your horse carrying himself in a good posture to condition his body properly. The horse's neck is one specific feature that determines good posture. The way a horse carries his neck determines the way his entire body moves, because the position of the neck determines the reflexes in the rest of the body. Why? In part, because nerve centers in the spinal column near the top of the neck act as a control center for reflexes that affect movement in the entire body. Pioneering studies in the past few decades have shown that nerves in the horse's neck and the "attitude" of the neck itself govern the entire body.

This is true of most animals, humans included. Think for a moment how your own neck (posture, tension, pain) affects the rest of your body and movement. Try sticking your head out in front of you like a turtle rather than balancing it correctly over your body and feel how this posture presses down on your shoulders and strains your upper back. Now try tensing your neck and clenching your jaw while you walk around. You see how the rest of your body is affected; how your back

muscles are changed and, therefore, your way of moving is altered?

It is similar with horses. When a horse braces his neck — either in response to bit pressure or through general resistance — he creates muscle contractions throughout his entire body. Studies show that, in this instance, flexor and extensor muscles contract at the same time. These muscles should contract independently, never at the same time. When they contract simultaneously, it causes continuous tension in surrounding joints.

On the other hand, if a horse neither braces his neck nor uses it in a stretched fashion, it is no better for his posture and carriage. Although he may not be experiencing contradictory muscle contractions, he is not engaging the control center for his body's correct muscle reflexes in a way that creates good posture. For the rest of the body to come into the proper balance, the neck must be in just the right position and carried with just the right tone. The illustrations that follow provide compelling insight into how neck posture can affect the rest of the skeleton, either positively or negatively.

Both cross-sections below are of horses the exact same size; however, the horse on the right appears to be shorter. The difference in height is explained by how the horse carries his torso between the shoulder blades. When a horse does not use his neck in an elongated manner, such as the horse on the right, his torso is carried low between his shoulder blades, which produces overstretching in some muscles and overshortening in others, creating the dropped torso.

A horse who uses his neck correctly, however, appears "bigger" over time because the shoulder girdle muscles are able to elevate the torso between the shoulder blades. This leads to well-developed back muscles, strong abdominal muscles, and elastic ligament connections.

Determining the Correct Neck Position

The drawing at the top of the next page shows a horse with an exemplary neck position. The activity of his neck has engaged his ring of muscles, which means he is well aligned and his hind legs are being pulled under his body. This horse makes himself stronger and more supple with every stride.

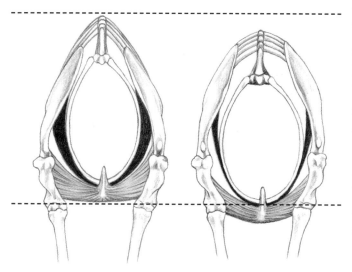

When a horse carries his neck incorrectly for a long time, it can lead to skeletal changes, like the dropped torso shown on the right.

This does not mean, however, that this horse has to ride in exactly this same posture every day. Some days he will have a little less energy or perhaps he will be stiff and his posture will need to be adjusted accordingly. That is perfectly fine as long as he still remains in a posture that is beneficial.

As an analogy, think of a human going to yoga class. Most of the time, she might be able to bend all the way over and touch her toes. But some days, she might be a little stiff for whatever reason and would need to strain to touch her toes all the way. Instead, she should bend over only far enough to touch her shins or even her knees. This stretching, while in fact not as extreme as that of the previous day, is still beneficial to her. It is the same with horses.

Range of Correct Motion

To keep my students from becoming too fixated on one exact posture, I like to show them that there is a range over which their horses can carry their necks and still create the proper reflexes in the rest of their bodies.

Keep these illustrations in mind in your own riding. Try to find your horse's range of beneficial carriage for his neck and figure out how to position him within that range on a day-to-day basis. To determine your horse's optimal range, learn to feel where you need to position his neck for him to lift his back under your seat. When he is lifting his back, you should feel that he seems wider underneath you or that your saddle is suddenly sitting on a mound rather than in a valley.

Once you feel his back lift up, play around with lowering his neck 3 to 4 more inches (8–10 cm). If your horse can maintain the same rhythm, without rushing, with his neck slightly lower, you have found his range for carrying his neck well.

This horse's neck is stretching forward from his shoulders and is neither forced nor slack. With his neck in this posture, the rest of his body is working properly.

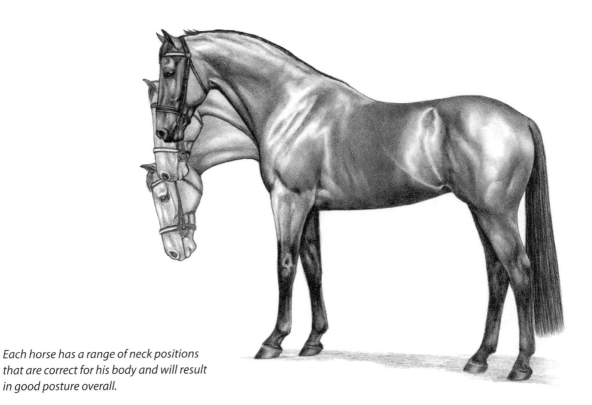

Each horse has a range of neck positions that are correct for his body and will result in good posture overall.

Horses have a common tendency to carry their necks slightly to one side rather than perfectly straight in front of their bodies. This is similar to the way in which many people walk or sit with one shoulder slightly higher than the other. When the horse moves with his neck like this, he is not using his hind legs evenly. With the mass of his head and neck (weighing roughly 250 pounds [113 kg]) to one side, his hind legs have to push unequally to compensate for the lack of balance. They are not able to push evenly under the body because the load that they are carrying is not straight!

Because it is slight, this asymmetry in the neck often goes undetected for quite a while, which, in turn, creates long-standing asymmetries in the rest of the horse's body. If a large portion of the horse's spine is always carried out of alignment with the rest of the body, any muscling or fitness will automatically be asymmetrical. Many riders refer to their horses as "one-sided," meaning that they perform better or are easier to ride when traveling either clockwise or counterclockwise. In reality, horses are *made* one-sided by being allowed to travel with their necks not centered in the middle of their bodies.

It can take some time to learn to see, both from the ground and in the saddle, when a horse is not carrying his neck in the middle of his body. What follows is a brief tutorial with drawings to start developing your eye. Your feel for straightness when mounted will follow with experience.

IS HIS NECK STRAIGHT?

To keep things simple, I tell riders to focus on two qualifiers: the horse's pectorals and ears. First, when the horse is moving, observe whether his nose is aligned over the center of his pectorals. If so, his neck is being carried in the center of his body. Next, observe whether his ears are level or one appears slightly lower. If one is lower, he is twisting his head to one side and creating crookedness at the top of his neck.

Now let's look at some drawings. The following drawings show whether the respective horses are carrying their necks in the middle of their pectorals. They include horses of different breeds, disciplines, and in various postures. Remember that, regardless of their disciplines, each must travel with a straight neck. Otherwise, the rest of the body is twisted and develops asymmetrical muscling and loses balance.

◀ *This horse may appear at first to be carrying his weight evenly over all four legs. If he were truly straight, however, his neck and spine would be directly in the center of his body mass, meaning his nose would be aligned in front of the crease between his chest muscles (pectorals). In this horse's case, you can see that he has swung his neck to the left and is carrying it in front of his shoulder,* not *the middle of his body.*

▶ *This horse has swung his neck toward the right and is carrying it directly in front of his outside shoulder. Again, this is crooked movement. His spine is not in the center of his body!*

▲ *This horse is making a 20-meter circle to the left* and his spine is fairly well flexed in the direction of his travel. You'll notice, however, that he is traveling with his head cocked to the inside of the circle. Instead, his head and face should hang straight down from his ears. The way he is traveling here causes his inside neck muscles to brace, his poll to be twisted, and his bit pressure to be uneven, which makes his hind legs travel unevenly.

▲ *This horse is also making a 20-meter circle to the left* with his spine mostly flexed in the direction of travel, except that he is twisting his head and has become crooked through his poll, jaw, and upper spine. He has turned his nose so that his neck is bent in to the left and his head and poll are bent the opposite way. His hips are not level and he is restricting movement with his outside hind leg.

▶ *This horse is not overtly twisting his neck one way or the other;* consequently, he might appear straighter than the other ones. He is, however, traveling crookedly. He is leaning with his neck and shoulder weight to the left and, therefore, is not straight. A rider might describe him as feeling "stiff" to the left. In his movement, he is constantly drifting toward the left with his shoulder weight.

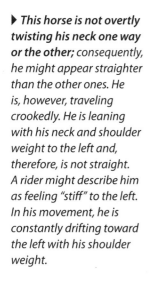

▶ *This horse is all jammed up!* With his spine twisting in an S like this, it is impossible for his hindquarters and front end to work together. A horse traveling in this manner will use each hind leg differently than the other, his hips will not be level, and his back will be crooked under the rider.

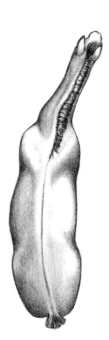

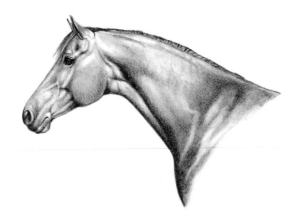

This illustration shows the development of proper muscling in the neck. The jugular groove is clearly defined, and the crest is nicely filled out from poll to withers.

This horse has too much muscle along the underside of his neck and not enough along the crest. Tension in his neck will restrict forward shoulder movement and create a braced jaw, causing stiffness throughout the back.

Let's Talk Muscles

Over time, a horse will develop musculature in his neck as he goes about his work properly. This musculature is roughly the same for all disciplines, although certain ones, such as dressage, result in heavier muscling. The basic outline of correct muscling, however, is no different. A look at how your horse's neck is filling out will tell you whether he is carrying himself in a good posture in his daily exercises.

There are certain muscles that *should* develop and others that *should not* develop. The bottom neck muscles (responsible for bracing the neck and holding it in a bad posture) should show no development, and the jugular groove should become clearly defined as a result. The crest should show muscling from poll to withers.

When the horse uses his neck correctly, he develops a little triangle muscle in front of the withers. This area should go from flat to looking somewhat puffed up, which indicates that the horse is stretching his neck correctly forward and thereby engaging his back and carrying his shoulders well.

Lack of development in this area indicates that the horse has been carrying his neck rigidly with a dropped back. One of the joys of early conditioning is seeing this hollow spot fill in with muscle! As the horse's posture improves, this triangle of muscle will show up.

Changing a poorly conformed or muscled neck takes time and patience.

A young horse with little or no muscling will change shape as he learns to carry his neck athletically.

30. Horizontal Frame Conditioning 94

31. Changing Speeds 95

32. Counter Canter Loops 97

33. Counter Canter Serpentines 98

34. Shoulder-In Repetitions 99

35. Shoulder-In Traveling Out (Manolo Mendez) 100

36. Striding In, Striding Out 101

NECK EXERCISES

30. Horizontal Frame Conditioning

Riding a horse in a good posture over his topline on straight lines guarantees that he pushes evenly from both hind legs as opposed to riding too many circles/turns, which causes the horse to overuse one side of his body. Riding the horse in an active gait while positioning his neck between the upper and lower ends of his range for healthy posture is one of the best things you can do for overall conditioning. It stretches and strengthens the entire back and topline. By varying his frame in front, the horse also flexes and engages his hindquarters accordingly to accommodate the different frames.

To do this work correctly, you want to ride the horse with a rein length that allows his poll and withers to be at the same height so that his body posture is horizontal to the ground. This is a useful exercise to insert into any regular training session or it can be used as a training session itself.

How Do I Do This?

1. Begin by trotting your horse in a "horizontal frame," meaning his poll and withers are at the same height and his neck is horizontal to the ground like a table.

2. When you feel he is reaching into the bit and you have good contact, begin to shorten the reins half an inch at a time.

3. Shorten the reins a total of about 2 inches (5 cm) or until the horse's poll is now the highest point on his body. Depending on his height, his ears might now be relatively level with your chest.

4. Keep the trot active and ride in this frame about 15 seconds.

5. Gradually let the reins slide through your fingers a half inch at a time until the horse is in a frame with his poll *lower* than his withers.

6. Ride 15 seconds in this frame.

7. Repeat the whole sequence several times in each direction.

8. When you are performing it well, also ride it at the canter.

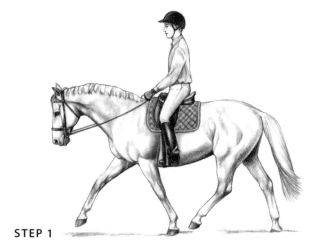

STEP 1

STEP 3

TIP FOR SUCCESS: If at any point while you are adjusting the reins, either longer or shorter, your horse becomes fidgety with the contact or drops it, stop at *exactly* that length of rein and ride forward until you regain his connection to your hand.

31. Changing Speeds

The moment of transitioning up to an extended gait is the most taxing, and strengthening, part of the transition. Once a horse reaches an extended gait, it is fairly easy for his body to sustain it. But the moment of pushing himself up into the extended pace is the critical period of conditioning. The play between two speeds also increases oxygen and blood flow to his muscles, which improves his range of motion.

How Do I Do This?

1. Choose either a working trot or working canter; this exercise is beneficial in only those two gaits.

2. Proceed in your working gait on either a very large circle or straightaway.

3. Making sure your horse is in a good posture, extend your gait.

4. Remain in the extended pace at least as long as you were in the working gait so that if you rode three-quarters of a lap around the arena in the working canter, extend the canter for the same distance.

5. Make a *gradual* downward transition to the working gait. It is important to gradually downshift from the extended pace so that the horse has a few strides to gather himself, keep his back round, and draw his hind legs underneath his body rather than making an abrupt transition where he stiffens his back.

6. Repeat numerous times in both trot and canter. Some riders make the mistake of riding this exercise only a few times in each direction. But it is only effective as a conditioning tool when the horse is pushed enough to take more oxygen into his body.

TIPS FOR SUCCESS: If you make the transitions too close together without the time to establish a clear rhythm in each pace, the horse will compromise the posture of his topline. Be sure to maintain a good posture in the horse throughout the entire exercise, otherwise it is fruitless.

Here's the big caveat for this exercise: allow the horse's neck to lengthen forward when you transition to the extended gait. If you do not, his body will remain blocked in the extension. He may indeed move his legs faster, but his topline will not be as engaged as it needs to be. His neck should reach more out from the shoulder (about the width of your hand) when you extend and then come back to you when you transition down to the working gait again.

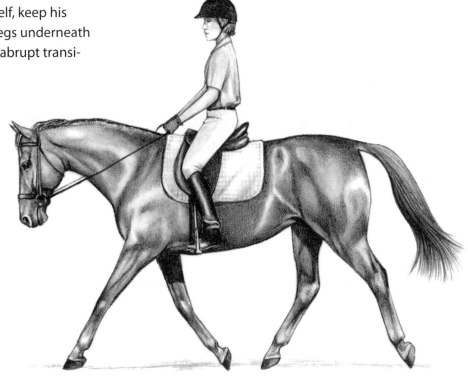

Counter Canter Overview

There is an immense difference between a correctly ridden counter canter and simply riding a horse on the wrong lead. In a correct counter canter, the horse should exhibit foremost a clear shifting of his weight to the hindquarters, an unrushed rhythm, and an even bend from poll to tail in the direction of his lead.

A correctly ridden counter canter is a wonderful bodybuilding tool because it asks more of the horse's musculature than do other gaits. First, it asks more of the horse's comfort zone in terms of his balance and, therefore, asks him to use his body to accommodate that difference in balance.

Second, when the exercise is ridden properly, the horse must tuck his pelvis underneath him, thereby strengthening his lower back. In counter canter, the horse's hips articulate and carry more torque than in regular canter, becoming stronger and more supple.

If you or your horse is inexperienced with counter canter, do yourself a favor and get some instruction. Some people fear that this is too advanced an exercise and wait too long to teach their horses. Truthfully, if your horse can execute a balanced regular canter on both leads, then you are ready to work on counter canter.

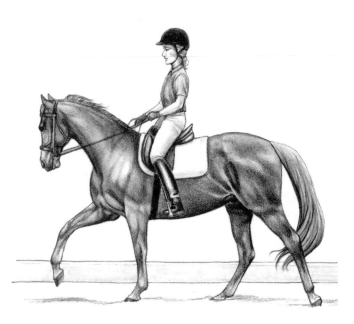

This horse is demonstrating a correct, balanced counter canter. Any exercise undertaken in this posture and rhythm will yield gymnastic benefit.

This horse is simply cantering on the wrong lead. You can tell this by observing that his weight is pushed over his front legs, he appears to be scrambling for balance, and his posture is disorganized.

32. Counter Canter Loops

This exercise is suitable for horses who have no formal training in counter canter. You do, however, need a fairly large arena to be productive. With a small arena, your horse will not have room to execute the pattern in a relaxed manner with a swinging rib cage.

How Do I Do This?

1. Begin by cantering on the right lead. Execute a few large circles on one end of your arena to establish a clear and consistent rhythm.

2. Leaving your circle, ride through the corner and then immediately peel off the rail toward the center of the arena.

3. When you are about 10 feet (3 m) from the rail, ride straight ahead for about 7 feet (2.1 m). Make sure your horse goes straight at this point. That is the test of his balance.

4. Guide him back to the rail in time for your next corner.

5. Instead of doing another shallow loop right away, ride straight down the following long side of your arena. This gives your horse the chance to get his hind legs balanced straight under his body again before repeating the exercise.

6. Practice in both directions.

TIPS FOR SUCCESS: If the horse changes his posture or his rhythm, make your loop even more shallow or "flatter" until you can ride it without fluctuations.

Be precise with your geometry because the difference in loop sizes taxes your horse's postural muscles distinctly.

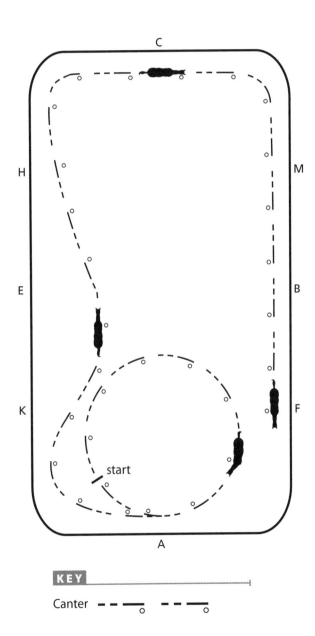

KEY

Canter

33. Counter Canter Serpentines

In this variation on the previous exercise (32. Counter Canter Loops), pay attention to your horse's rhythm as you do each loop. Starting with the shallowest serpentine, make sure he is maintaining a consistent rhythm before going on to the deeper ones.

How Do I Do This?

1. Develop a working canter on the right lead and begin by riding alternately between a 20-meter-diameter circle and a 15-meter-diameter circle, to get the horse on your aids for changing the size of his bend.

2. When you've established a consistent canter, ride the first bend in the diagram. Make sure your horse's rhythm, bend, and posture remain even throughout.

3. Ride straight down the following long side of the arena, then begin the next bend.

4. Once you are consistent on this pattern, ride the third one.

5. Play around with the different patterns, tracing each one with your horse and alternating between them.

6. Work in both directions.

TIP FOR SUCCESS: Follow the suggested geometry precisely. The shape of the pattern determines whether the horse balances himself correctly or is going about the work in a compromised posture.

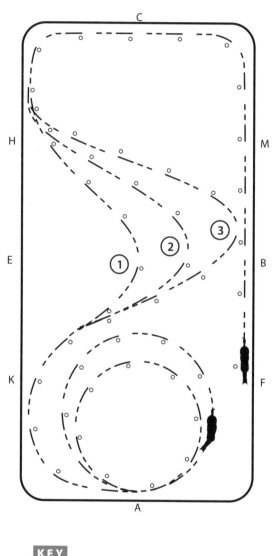

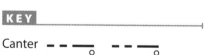

KEY

Canter - - —   - - —

34. Shoulder-In Repetitions

This exercise improves three areas at once: cardiovascular fitness, hindquarter strength, and shoulder looseness and mobility. It is similar to a human workout routine where several reps of a particular exercise are performed with the intention of progressively stressing a muscle group.

Note: You will need a heart-rate monitor to accurately assess your horse's stress level.

How Do I Do This?

1. In an arena or flat surface with good, level footing, begin in an active working trot traveling clockwise. Note your horse's heart rate on the heart monitor after 4 minutes.

2. Maintaining a steady rhythm, execute 10 steps of shoulder-in, taking note of the horse's heart rate as he moves over.

3. Note how many strides of shoulder-in it takes until his heart rate rises noticeably (20 beats or more above his normal heart rate for a normal working trot). For most horses, it will take just four or five strides. That number of strides is the "set" that will be repeated throughout the workout.

4. Once you have determined the number of strides in your set, continue trotting around the arena riding various simple patterns (big circles, diagonals, and figure eights). Every 60 seconds, execute a shoulder-in set.

5. After each set, continue riding simple patterns for 60 seconds.

6. Repeat this cycle for 5 to 10 minutes in both directions, depending on your horse's skill with shoulder-in. Keep checking the heart rate to ensure you are getting a consistent rise in heart rate for each shoulder-in set.

TIP FOR SUCCESS: Maintain the same energy and intensity level throughout this exercise — it's an active one!

35. Shoulder-In Traveling Out

Contributed by **Manolo Mendez**, Cofounder of the Royal School of Equestrian Arts in Jerez, Spain

This exercise is similar to the leg-yield. It differs (and derives more gymnastic benefit), however, by keeping the horse's spine in the alignment of shoulder-in. That spinal flexion leads to suppling, strengthening, and balance. It allows for more lateral range of motion in the limbs as well as stretching in the shoulder girdle. In addition to strengthening the hind legs, it also provides a great stretch for his front end because it causes his scapula to slide in an exaggerated motion sideways across his chest wall.

How Do I Do This?

1. Begin in an active working trot traveling clockwise around your arena.

2. At one end of the arena, ride a 15-meter circle to maintain your rhythm and establish an inside bend throughout your horse's spine. Keep an active tempo.

3. Ride a quarter of the way again around the circle and then gently displace the horse's front end with your right leg in the direction of the rail. You should end up with a slight diagonal slant in the horse's body toward the rail.

4. Ask him to move sideways from your right leg toward that rail while ensuring that his forehand remains ahead of his haunches.

5. As you travel slightly sideways to the rail, keep the horse's spine bent to the right. His body should feel "curled" around your right leg.

6. When you reach the rail, accelerate the trot for two or three strides to push the horse's hind legs back underneath him after any potential trailing behind in the sideways movement.

7. Travel around the entire arena and then repeat.

TIP FOR SUCCESS: Your horse needs to be moderately well schooled in shoulder-in, where he travels straight while bending himself and displacing his shoulders to the inside of the arena, moving his inside front leg onto a separate track from his hind leg.

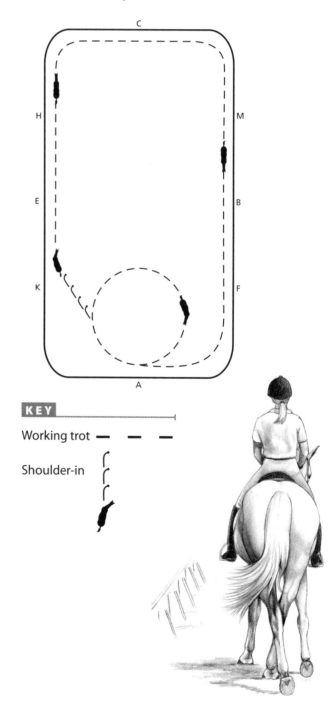

KEY

Working trot ‒ ‒ ‒

Shoulder-in

36. Striding In, Striding Out

This exercise asks a lot of your horse's hindquarter flexibility and strength — particularly hamstrings, stifle, and abdominal regions — because it varies the length of stride with obstacles and requires good tone for the horse to keep his balance while doing so. It is beneficial only if done accurately and cleanly, without the horse tripping or overextending over poorly spaced poles.

How Do I Do This?

1. Develop a brisk working trot.

2. Aim straight over the first set of four poles.

3. About 3 feet (1 m) before you reach the first pole, ask your horse to slow down a little and shorten his stride.

4. Proceed over the poles in just four strides. Your horse should not take any strides between the poles or try to cover two poles at once.

5. Proceed straight to the next set of poles and start to push his trot more actively forward.

6. Ride over the second set of poles visualizing an extended trot. Again, your horse should cover the poles in just four strides, no more and no less.

TIP FOR SUCCESS: Some riders have trouble feeling whether their horses are sneaking in extra strides between the poles or the poles are sufficiently far apart to require that the horse stretch and extend his stride beyond his normal length. If you need assistance at first, a ground person will be able to tell you what's happening with your horse's stride and can move poles around for you as necessary.

Before you begin, set up eight ground poles according to the diagram. Place the first four poles spaced apart at a distance that is roughly 1 to 2 inches (2.5–5 cm) shorter than the length of your horse's normal stride in the trot. After this set of four poles, leave a 32.8-foot (10 m) gap and then set up four more poles, this time spacing the poles at a distance 1 to 2 inches (2.5–5 cm) longer than the length of your horse's normal stride.

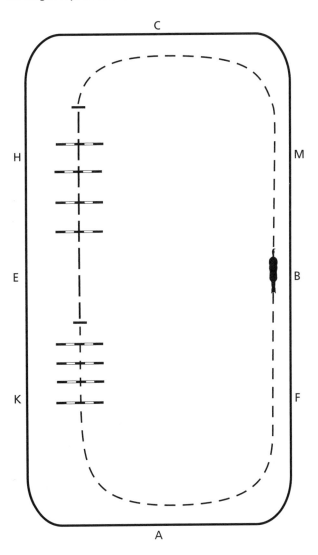

KEY

Working trot — — —

Extended trot —— —— ——

Transition —

THE STIFLE IS CRITICAL

MOST RIDERS IN ANY DISCIPLINE know the value of sound hocks for ensuring the best performance from their horses. Too few riders, however, recognize the equally critical role of the horse's stifle. The stifle joint is located where the hind leg connects to the horse's torso. Built and functioning almost exactly like the human knee, it consists of a kneecap and three patella ligaments, with the horse's quadricep muscles attaching to it. Tone in these ligaments and muscles allows the horse's hind legs to properly lift and swing forward under his body. The stifle joint generates push and thrust during each stride. Simply put: it pulls the hind limbs forward. Without it, the horse's hind limbs would move straight up and down like broomsticks and never come forward.

In terms of dressage work, the stifle's action translates to the development of impulsion and increased articulation of the hind limbs. In terms of jumping horses or those needing to momentarily compress their hindquarters (e.g. Western reining or working cows), fitness and elasticity of the stifle allow the hindquarters to lower as they need to. Failure of the stifle (through lack of fitness) can lead to injury or create strain on other areas of the horse's musculoskeletal system.

When a horse's stifles are not working properly, his hind legs will trail out behind his body rather than being pulled forward under his mass by his stifle ligaments as they should be. This causes problems. How the horse's hind legs move when you ride him determines how he uses his pelvis and hindquarters. And how he uses his entire body determines whether he becomes stronger as opposed to stiffer and more broken down each day you ride.

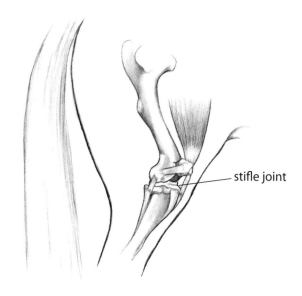

stifle joint

Stifle weakness derails many performance horses.

Assessing Stifle Function

Stifle ligaments are like the belts in your car. If it isn't tight and working properly, a belt can cause problems such as slipping out of gear, poor steering, failure to regulate the engine, and so on. In horses, loose, unfit stifles frequently result in resistance to engagement (including turns and circles), shortened steps, and swinging the hind legs, most visibly at the walk. In addition, horses will flinch if you manipulate a tender stifle muscle or ligament.

Here are some ways to determine whether a horse is having difficulties with his stifle:

Walking Away

Observe the horse as it is walked straight away from you. Do his hind feet go straight forward under his barrel or do they swing outward in tiny arcs each time they move forward?

Under Saddle

Observe the horse both walking and trotting under saddle. Dragging the hind feet forward in continuous contact with the ground without lifting them out of the footing is a clear sign of weak stifles. A horse that becomes fussy cantering circles is often compromised in the stifles.

A horse with inherently weak or loose stifles will also show a lack of engagement, despite the rider's best efforts to get his hindquarters pushing. These horses lack any spring in their gaits and their hind limbs are not drawn forward under the body at each stride.

Walking Downhill

Watch him negotiate a downhill grade at a slow walk. A horse with weak stifles will tend to shift his hips to one side and "crab walk," while also dragging his hind feet behind him. If the horse allows you to straighten him while proceeding down the hill, his stifle weakness is not too severe. If the horse puts up a fight when asked to travel straight, however, his stifles are most likely too weak, from injury or because of genetics, to ever be made fit for any rigorous discipline.

WATCH OUT FOR STIFLE WEAKNESS

If you're in the market for a horse, don't overlook the stifles! Many buyers have the hocks radiographed, but they may not realize that weak stifles are potentially an even greater liability. There is nothing you can do to make a badly conformed horse overcome stifle weakness.

Examine the placement of the stifle joint. It should not point backwards behind the horse, but rather be located nearly directly under the hip. Its placement should allow the horse at rest to stand with his hind feet directly under his hips — *not* trailing out behind his pelvis.

Some breeds are more predisposed to conformational weakness in the stifle area, at least for the purposes of rigorous hind-end work. Some Thoroughbreds, for example, have been bred for "open joints": straighter stifles, with a steeper angle between the hind legs and the body. This straighter leg is believed to help track racehorses achieve faster speeds, but demands from other disciplines will unduly stress the joint because a straight stifle causes greater laxity of patella ligaments.

In addition, because many warmblood breeds grow so rapidly as youngsters, their joints can become "sloppy," meaning the ligaments have been stretched out early to accommodate rapid growth and will need time to tighten back up and develop strength.

Be on the lookout for horses with joints that are large compared with those of the average horse; you will need to take more time strengthening the hind end to allow those ligaments to tighten properly. Remember: Ligaments can take longer to strengthen than muscles.

The Flexion Test

Flex the horse's hind leg(s) by lifting the hoof slightly off the ground. Then rub and gently squeeze the stifle area. If there is a "grinding" noise in this flexed position or you feel sponginess around the stifle when rubbing, it is an indication of an unstable knee. Loosening the horse's hamstrings — using the stretches in this book — will help to stabilize the stifle. The stifle is the joint most prone to cause pain when a horse is not worked properly!

KEY POINT

> Without proper functioning and conditioning in the stifle joint, stifle ligaments, and stifle muscles, any sport horse will be derailed from optimal performance.

Building Strength in the Stifle

The exercises given here are extremely useful for conditioning a horse's hind end and, specifically, his stifles. First, however, you must choose the correct rhythm for your horse. This is similar to choosing the right speed at which to perform your own human workout. Go too fast or too slowly and you get no results. Only the correct rhythm will yield the results we are looking for.

Because horses are quadrupeds, you must choose a rhythm for your horse that enables his front *and* back ends to put in equal amounts of effort at every stride, which means he moves with even spacing between both pairs of legs. Sometimes when a rider asks the horse to move too vigorously forward (in a quick tempo), the horse's front legs will take larger and larger steps, meaning they spread apart more at every stride.

Weak stifles can be made stronger, but ones with chronic functional issues cannot be improved.

But when they spread wider, the horse tips onto his forehand too much and his hind legs cannot catch up with the movement. The horse ends up moving more quickly, but as the front legs take longer and longer strides, the back legs take choppier and choppier strides. The back and front ends move at different speeds and in a disjointed manner. This indicates that the horse's two ends are not in harmony and, therefore, not in balance. Exercising an unbalanced horse produces only strain and stiffness.

Depending on your horse's size, age, and physical stiffness, you need to exercise him in a rhythm that is beneficial for *him*. Because of their age, stiffness, or lack of balance, some horses need to be ridden in a much slower tempo because that is the speed at which they can achieve equal spacing between front and back pairs of legs.

In this way, his body can work harmoniously and productively, not just on the forehand with excessive stress to the front legs. On the other hand, some naturally elastic and supple horses need to be pushed vigorously forward to achieve the right rhythm where the front and hind ends are in harmony.

KEY POINT To determine the correct rhythm for your horse, have someone watch you ride or videotape you riding in all three gaits. Look for the speed at which your horse's front and back ends look as though they're making the same amount of effort.

Working in Deep Sand

Working a horse in deep sand significantly taxes his body and can be extremely beneficial to the conditioning of his entire ligament system, in addition to his stifles. If used responsibly, it can build him up substantially. You can, however, easily overstrain your horse, so heed the following precautions:

- Avoid boggy, heavy, or uneven sand that would risk ligament tears or twisted ankles;

instead, seek out the depth and type of sand you would find alongside the ocean during low tide — two inches deep and compacted, not loose and sliding around.
- Start easy and build up; beginning with no longer than 10 minutes of work and add 5 minutes each week.
- Trotting is the most productive pace in which to ride through sand; in the walk and canter, a horse's hind end will most likely trail out behind him in deeper footing.
- Listen to your horse's breathing and when his respiration elevates, give him a break until his breathing returns to normal; otherwise, he will not be oxygenating his muscles properly.
- Always check the horse's lower legs for heat following the workout.

Working on Uneven Terrain

Riding up and down hills, no matter the size, will greatly improve your horse's hind-end strength, although much depends on *how* your horse negotiates the terrain. Little fitness will be achieved if he goes about it in a bad posture, poor rhythm, or crookedly. For work at the walk and trot, heed the following suggestions. When you're ready to work at the canter, see Cantering on Uneven Terrain, page 113.

Use Correct Rein Length

Hold the reins at a length that keeps the poll and withers at the same height so that the horse's topline is round, rather than allowing the horse to "flop" over onto his forehand while riding hills.

Ride Hills Perfectly Straight

It's important to go straight up and down. Don't zigzag or allow the horse to crab walk; he must bring his hind legs straight forward under his body. Riding up and down a gradual slope is just as worthwhile as working on a steep one.

Mind Your Speed

The *slower* you ride uphill, the more strength you gain in the hind end; a horse does not build much strength by scrambling quickly up a hill, but *does* gain strength from walking or trotting slowly uphill.

Seek Out Rolling Terrain

Find a spot (even an open field will do) where you can maintain a single consistent rhythm with the horse while negotiating up and down; this is invaluable for the hind legs as well as the horse's balance.

Mind Your Own Posture

Some riders try to "help" their horses up a hill by throwing themselves too far forward in the saddle. This actually puts additional stress on your mount's front legs. The best thing is to sit as tall as possible so that your own balance is upright, allowing the horse to move unencumbered without your additional weight on his forehand.

Don't Forget Transitions

When hill riding, execute a transition (walk-trot-walk) now and then to increase the workload. Your horse will need to shift his balance as well as push off even more from the hindquarters for a few strides.

KEEPING AN EYE ON TAIL CARRIAGE

Remember that a horse's tail is an extension of his spine. Therefore, how a horse carries his tail indicates the state of his back. The attitude of the tail should be closely examined by rider and trainer to determine the quality of how a horse uses his back.

When a riding horse is working with his back properly engaged, his dock should be carried horizontally to the ground and the tail itself should hang slightly arched and swing freely in rhythm with the movement of his hind limbs.

A clamped down or motionless tail that does not swing at the bottom indicates a stiff horse with a tense back, perhaps due to soreness, cold muscles, or poor training. A limp tail, which seems to hang with no tone in the dock, indicates very slack back muscles. Asymmetrical muscling along the horse's back will result in the tail being carried to one side.

37. Trotting Poles in an Arc 108

38. Pick-up Sticks 109

39. Lifting the Hind Legs 110

40. Bringing the Hind Legs Forward 111

41. Stepping Over Slowly 112

42. Cantering on Uneven Terrain 113

43. In and Out Leg-Yielding (Becky Hart) 114

STIFLE EXERCISES

37. Trotting Poles in an Arc

Riding over ground poles requires that the horse flex his stifles while maintaining a steady pace, thereby creating additional strength. Incorporate one day of work over poles per week into your performance horse's routine. Mark out a 20-meter circle in your arena and place five ground poles in a fan shape on the arc of the circle. The middle of each ground pole should be a stride apart from the next.

How Do I Do This?

1. Walk your horse over the ground poles to ensure that the spacing is correct for his stride. Remain on the arc of the circle while traversing exactly over the *middle* of each pole. Do not drift to the outside edge!

2. Once your horse is going well in the walk, ride the ground pole circle in the rising trot.

3. Repeat several times in each direction, keeping an active trot and maintaining an inside bend through your horse's neck and rib cage.

TIP FOR SUCCESS: Make a note if one direction of the exercise seems more difficult than the other. This indicates asymmetry in your horse's way of going, which you can address with targeted stretching after the session.

VARIATION

Ride the same pattern, except raise the poles 6 inches (15 cm) off the ground with jump standards or cones. Ride with a slightly forward and light seat.

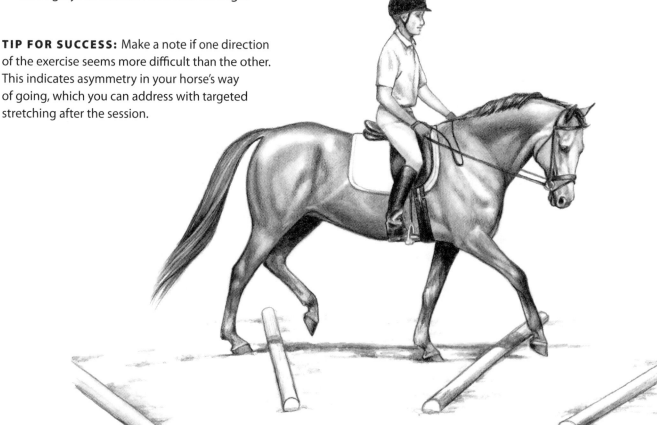

38. Pick-up Sticks

For this exercise, you will need a number (at least 10, but more is better) of ground poles or large-diameter PVC pipes, which are lighter and easier to handle. Scatter them around a 20-meter area so that some of them are lying across each other and others are away from the group in a random pattern. The random spacing and heights of the poles once all spread out force the horse to adjust his stride and footfall. This exercise improves the horse's coordination and proprioception (the signals from his nerves to move his limbs in certain ways). A more-coordinated horse is capable of better balance and alignment.

How Do I Do This?

1. Mount your horse and find a line from one side of the area to the other through that mess of poles.

2. For safety, walk the line first.

3. Once at the other side, turn around and find a different way back.

4. If you are finding success, then try jogging a few steps.

5. Find as many routes through the pole pile as possible, or make up little patterns.

TIP FOR SUCCESS: Keep only a loose rein contact and, as much as possible, don't interfere with your horse. Point him where you want to go, sit back, and let him find his way. You are teaching him to balance himself.

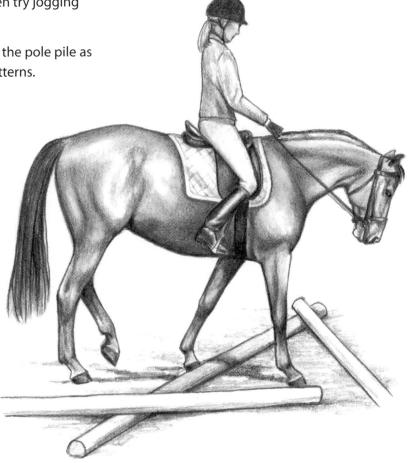

39. Lifting the Hind Legs

Working the horse from the ground allows you to teach him to bring his hind legs farther under his body. If you incorporate work in hand regularly into your workouts, you will eventually notice that the horse begins to improve his overall standing posture at rest. He will begin to stand with his hind feet drawn squarely under his body as opposed to "parked out" behind him. Although it may appear inanely simple, this exercise strengthens the horse's hindquarters and is highly effective because it does so without the added burden of a rider.

How Do I Do This?

1. Position your horse so that he is standing squarely and quietly along a fence, with his weight evenly distributed over all four feet. (The fence serves to keep him balanced and straight laterally.)

2. Ask your horse to relax his head and neck so that his back is rounded, not hollow. Ideally, have him lower his head so that his poll and withers are at the same height.

3. Keeping his neck stretched, reach back with your longe whip or a bamboo cane and gently tap his near hind leg until he raises that foot off the ground.

4. Change direction along the fence and repeat with the opposite hind leg.

5. Gradually progress to having him flex the leg and hold the foot in the air for up to 10 seconds (do this by gently tapping again when he tries to put the foot back down on the ground).

TIPS FOR SUCCESS: Every horse responds differently to whip cues, depending on where he is or isn't sensitive on his legs. Some horses will lift their hind legs when asked with a light touch near the middle of the cannon bone, but others will be more responsive to the area just below the hock or on the inside of their legs. Play around to see what works best for your horse and praise him whenever he even attempts to do what you're asking.

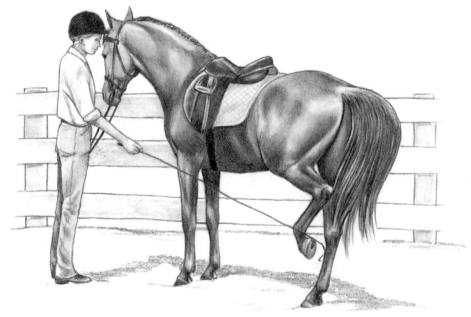

You can do this work with your horse outfitted in a plain halter, bridle, or longeing cavesson. You will need a longe whip or long bamboo cane.

40. Bringing the Hind Legs Forward

A horse does not always need to be in motion to become stronger. This exercise strengthens the ring of muscles — particularly the back and hindquarters — by putting the horse in a different posture and creating a deep stretch over his topline.

How Do I Do This?

1. Position your horse so that he is standing squarely and quietly along a fence, with his weight evenly distributed over all four feet. (The fence serves to keep him balanced and straight laterally.)

2. Ask him to stretch his neck toward the ground by using light downward pressure on his cavesson or reins.

3. Keeping your left hand near his nose/reins in case he tries to brace upward out of the posture, reach back with your right hand and tickle just behind his girth area to ask him to engage his belly and round his back.

4. Now reach back with your whip and ask him to bring one hind foot farther forward under his body. Do this by gently tapping behind his cannon bone. Some horses respond better to being tapped on the inside of the leg.

5. Keep your horse stretching forward with his neck. Then ask each hind leg to keep inching forward under the body.

6. Once you have achieved the desired stance, ask him to stand quietly in this posture for 10 to 15 seconds and then allow him to simply be "at ease" before moving forward.

TIPS FOR SUCCESS: As always when dealing with your horse's balance, take time to develop the exercise day by day. Be satisfied with a little progress at a time and reward often.

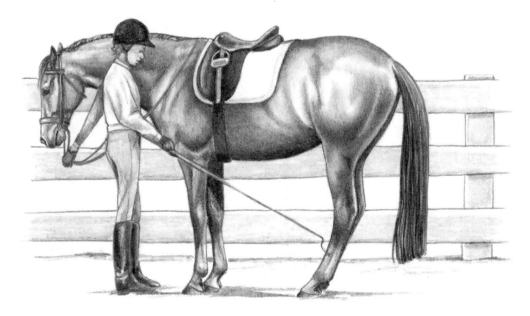

You will need a plain halter, bridle, or longeing cavesson, as well as a longe whip or long bamboo cane.

41. Stepping Over Slowly

This exercise serves as both physical therapy for an injured/weak stifle and as conditioning for a decent stifle. The slow flexing motion creates strength and pliability in the muscles and ligaments of the horse's knee.

How Do I Do This?

1. Place a tall but relatively soft object on level ground (an arena is ideal, but a driveway will suffice).

2. Lead your horse straight up to the object and halt.

3. Ask him to step very slowly over the object, one foot at a time.

4. Once he picks up his hind leg to step over the object, try to make him hesitate a few seconds so that he prolongs the motion of clearing his leg over to the other side.

5. Repeat a few times back and forth.

TIPS FOR SUCCESS: The crucial element of this exercise is doing it *as slowly as possible*. This is what builds strength in the stifle. Rushing over the obstacle will have no benefit.

Use an object about 2-feet (0.6 m) high that will make your horse pull his leg up to walk over. It should be suitably soft in case he gets worried and steps on or kicks it. A hay bale works fine, as does a collapsible mesh laundry basket with some added weight to keep it in place.

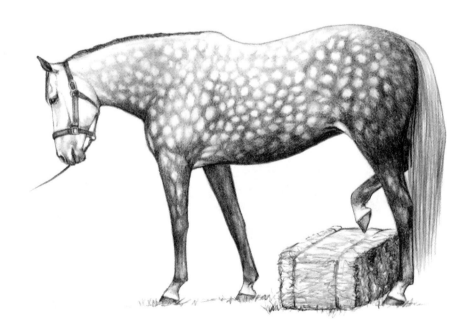

42. Cantering on Uneven Terrain

Tackle this exercise for major conditioning benefits. The difference in terrain asks more of his musculature as he finds his balance on uneven ground. This exercise is only beneficial if the terrain is *rolling*, not steep. If the terrain is too steep or the footing too poor, the horse will need to struggle for his balance, which will result in braced muscles and no conditioning benefit.

Note: This exercise assumes that your horse can already canter in a balanced manner in good posture. If he cannot, stick to working in the arena for now.

How Do I Do This?

1. Warm up by walking your horse vigorously on a long rein out in the open space.

2. Pick up a canter on either lead and start by cantering the gentlest slopes at first, cutting across the downward grades at 45-degree angles.

3. Gradually make your approach to the downward grades steeper.

4. Keep the speed of the canter consistent regardless of the grade of the terrain. At first, you may need a few strong half halts to show your horse not to change speeds when the terrain changes.

5. Keep doing this exercise for as long as possible. Don't quit after a few times around your open space; horses, as humans, generally improve on the exercise after they've been at it a while, have figured out where to put their feet, and have allowed themselves to relax into the movement.

TIPS FOR SUCCESS: Posture is critical in this exercise. You want to maintain a light contact with the horse's mouth so that you can guide him back to a good frame if he tries to hollow out when losing his balance.

Try to ride the horse in this exercise with your reins about 2 inches (5 cm) longer than you would have them for normal arena riding. You want the horse's neck stretched out so he can use it to gain his balance over the terrain, without becoming either too high headed or too low with his neck or plodding around with too much weight on his front end.

Note how a difference in posture affects the horse in going about this exercise. When a horse uses his back and ring of muscles properly, as shown above, he becomes stronger thanks to the added resistance of terrain changes. When he travels in a bad posture, on the other hand, the jarring of the exercise taxes his joints and tendons.

43. In and Out Leg-Yielding

Contributed by **Becky Hart,** Three-Time World Champion, Endurance Riding

With its many components, this exercise combines the demands of lengthening/shortening stride and leg-yielding, so that two things are achieved: suppling the front and hind ends of the horse and strengthening the shoulder girdle muscles. In addition, it's a fun exercise in the company of other horses!

How Do I Do This?

1. Begin with your whole group of riders (ideally three to five) in single file, trotting down an open section of roadway (or arena). Maintain a horse's length spacing between all the horses in line.

2. When all the horses are sustaining the same speed, have the last horse in line leg-yield three steps to the left to come out of the single-file line and immediately extend the trot to pass all the other riders.

3. At the front of the line, slow down to regain the trotting tempo of the group.

4. Leg-yield three steps to the right to arrive back in the single-file line in lead position.

5. As soon as the first horse has established position back in the single-file line, the horse now at the end of the line repeats the sequence.

6. If possible, continue with this exercise for a couple of miles, or at least 15 minutes.

TIP FOR SUCCESS: Be sure the horses in the line maintain a steady and unchanging rhythm rather than racing the passing horse. This is critical to allow the passing horse a clear change of pace to the extended trot and then a clear transition back to a steady working trot. This extending and then reducing of pace is a large part of the exercise's value.

Ride good-quality leg-yields, applying the aids correctly to get a decent bend in your horse's spine and sufficient crossover in the front and hind limbs.

CHAPTER 8

TIME TO STRETCH

THE BENEFITS OF STRETCHING speak for themselves. A stretched, supple muscle is a stronger muscle. Stretching keeps the muscles and tendons loose, allowing joints to move more freely and the horse to travel through his paces with ease. And stretching helps to eliminate waste products from muscles, ridding the horse of stiffness or soreness.

If your horse lives in a box stall, stretches are best performed after your riding workout when his musculature is warm and not at risk of tearing or overstraining in a stretch. If your horse lives in a paddock with room to move around throughout the day, however, he will take well to the following stretches done at the beginning of a session. That way, the effect of the stretched muscles can be built upon during the riding session, yielding far greater results overall!

The Benefits of Massage

Muscle tightening begins as a small bit of knotted tissue, perhaps the size of your thumb. Left untreated, the tension does not remain isolated. Neighboring muscle groups begin to pick up the stress load and tightness starts to build. Tight muscles require assistance in the form of stretching/massage therapy to restore circulation and elasticity. Otherwise, the horse is exercising in a compromised manner and is at risk of increased stiffness and injury.

An equine massage therapist is a valuable resource for any performance program, even for the recreational horse. Not only does an occasional massage keep a horse's muscles in optimal condition, but a massage therapist can also become an insightful sounding board for you. By reading your horse's body, a therapist can inform you of important details such as where your horse is getting sore or whether you might be pushing him too hard. She can also give you feedback that his body feels great and is working well with the exercise regimen you've been doing.

In my own training work, equine "bodyworkers" are a critical part of the performance equation. I rely on them to tell me which parts of the horse's body feel good and which feel tight. Comparing their input to what I've been noticing in my training sessions helps me to better read each horse's threshold, saddle fit, enjoyment of our work, and other athletic assessments.

A massage therapist might not be in everyone's budget, even though he or she is a wonderful resource if you can afford it. Fortunately, a wealth of useful information is readily available for horse owners to develop and practice basic massage techniques themselves. In fact, I encourage you to do this even if you already use a massage therapist. Nothing is better for evaluating your horse's changing shape, feeling for heat, noting ticklish or sore spots, finding knotted tissue, and so on than learning a few simple massage techniques and applying them on a regular basis. You should have a very thorough knowledge of how your horse's body feels, and running your hands over him consistently is the best way to gain that knowledge and identify any trouble spots immediately. In the early stages, simple massage goes far in eradicating a problem before it worsens.

BASIC MASSAGE TECHNIQUES

You can easily teach yourself the three basic massage techniques: effleurage, compression, and direct pressure.

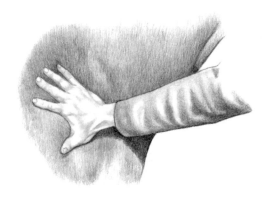

EFFLEURAGE

Slide an open, flat hand over the horse's skin and down the length of the muscle, feeling for tension, tightness, and abnormalities. Follow this with compression.

COMPRESSION

Target problem areas found during effleurage. Press into the muscle and rotate your hand in a half circle toward the horse's tail with a rhythmic, pumping action. Each individual horse will indicate how much or little pressure he prefers. With knotted tissue, apply direct pressure.

DIRECT PRESSURE

Press firmly into knotted tissue using your thumb or finger pad. Hold the same pressure for 30 seconds and release. Then, repeat for slightly longer. Do this a few times. Avoid particularly painful areas and hot or swollen spots.

44. Shoulder Rotation Stretch 118

45. Rear-Leg Circles 119

46. Pelvis Tucks 120

47. Poll Stretch 121

48. Hip Stretch 122

49. Shoulder Circles 123

50. Bladder Meridian Exercise for
Tension Release (Jim Masterson) 124

STRETCHING EXERCISES

44. Shoulder Rotation Stretch

Front leg stretches help relax and tone muscles in the forelegs and improve range of motion, especially the shoulder and elbow joints. These types of stretches improve the flow of energy throughout the entire horse. These subtle shoulder movements target the ascending and descending pectoral muscles — an area that helps move and stabilize the front legs and is commonly taxed by arena riding such as dressage or reining. Tension here creates choppy strides and limits lateral movement.

How Do I Do This?

1. Stand facing your horse's shoulder.

2. Clasp the leg above the knee and raise it just to the point of resistance, then release it slightly.

3. Gently rotate the leg three to five times in a 3-inch (8 cm) circle moving the leg forward and backward, not side to side.

4. Increase the diameter of your circle to 4 or 5 inches (10–13 cm) and repeat three to five times.

5. Increase the diameter of your circle to 6 or 7 inches (15–18 cm) and repeat.

6. Reverse the direction of the rotation, starting with a small circle as described above and increasing the diameter every three to five rotations.

7. Return your horse's hoof to its original position and repeat the entire sequence two or three times.

8. Repeat the sequence on his other front leg.

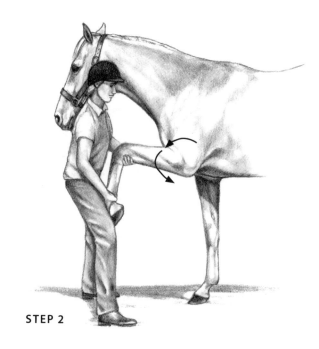

STEP 2

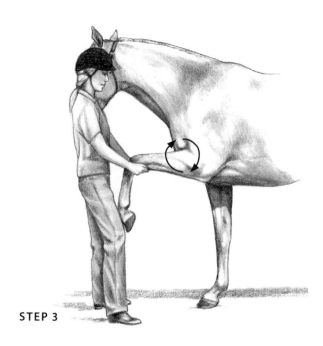

STEP 3

45. Rear-Leg Circles

This stretch targets the horse's hips and creates a gentle rocking motion in the pelvis, allowing the lower back to remain supple.

How Do I Do This?

1. Stand near your horse's right hip, facing his tail.

2. Bend over and place your right hand around the inside of his leg above the hock. Place your left hand on the back side of his fetlock.

3. Lift the leg off the ground and pull it forward several inches and then set the toe on the ground for a count of 3 seconds.

4. Slowly pull the leg to the outside and touch the hoof to the ground for another 3 seconds.

5. Push the leg behind the horse and touch the hoof to the ground for 3 seconds.

6. Rest the leg in its original position before repeating the sequence.

7. Repeat twice with each hind leg.

TIP FOR SUCCESS: Move slowly in this stretch. You do not want the horse to pull his leg up and away from you.

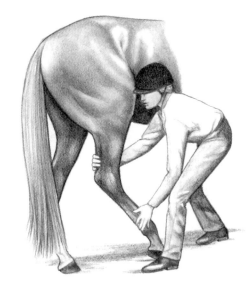

STEP 3

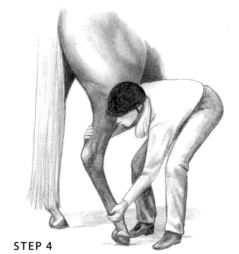

STEP 4

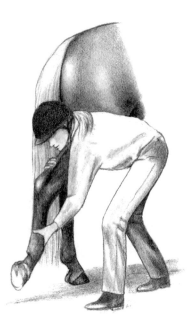

STEP 5

46. Pelvis Tuck

This exercise is more of a strength builder than a stretch. It demands the same response from the horse as when a human executes a sit-up. It is incredibly valuable for stretching the horse's back and lumbar region as well as toning the abdominals.

Note: You should not attempt this exercise if your horse is at all prone to kicking.

How Do I Do This?

1. Stand squarely behind your horse (make sure he knows you're there!).

2. Tuck the tips of each thumb just under the dock of his tail.

3. Extend your fingers straight up to form a "box" with your thumbs.

4. Apply direct pressure into the horse's buttocks muscle with the tips of your index fingers.

5. If the horse does not immediately tuck or "squat" his pelvis away from that pressure, try a light tickling or scratching motion.

6. Repeat at least twice.

TIP FOR SUCCESS: Some horses are very sensitive in this area and others are duller. You may need to alter your hand position to find your own horse's response.

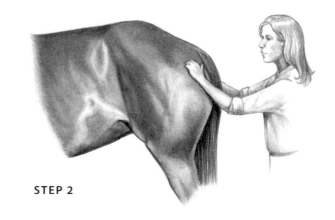

STEP 2

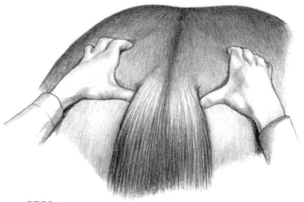

STEP 4

47. Poll Stretch

Some folks will regard this seemingly nondramatic stretch skeptically, disregarding its importance. To do so, however, would be to miss the significance of the horse's head-to-neck connection on the rest of his body. Tightness, stiffness, or crookedness at the horse's poll adversely affects the rest of his neck muscles and, therefore, his back muscles and ability of his hindquarters. An ill-stretched poll can be responsible for a horse refusing to canter on a specific lead, resisting certain aspects of work, avoiding the bit, and other issues.

How Do I Do This?

1. Stand alongside your horse just behind his jaw, facing forward.

2. Place your right hand on his neck just behind his poll and apply light pressure to prevent him from bending his neck toward you.

3. With your left hand, either hold the bridge of his nose or the halter nosepiece and draw just his head toward you. You want only his head to swivel toward you, while his neck remains straight. Be sure his ears and nostrils remain level.

4. Hold the stretch approximately 20 seconds then repeat on the other side.

TIPS FOR SUCCESS: If your horse has an old injury from pulling back, flipping over, or poor training, he may have inflammation in his poll and be resistant towards this stretch. Go easy at first and heed any adamant fussiness from your horse.

If your horse is at all tight on one side of his poll or upper neck, you will see him react to the stretch by sighing, licking his lips or chewing, or closing his eyes sleepily. If you see this, repeat another stretch on that side.

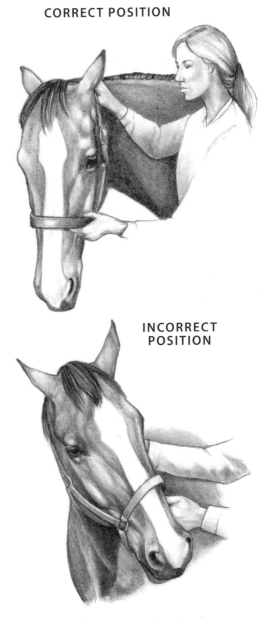

CORRECT POSITION

INCORRECT POSITION

You do not want the head and nose to tip toward you, as shown here.

48. Hip Stretch

Mobility in the hip joints increases the horse's range of motion because that is where the hind legs swing from. Tightness or restriction in this area will eventually lead to stiffness in the overall pelvis and produce shortened, choppy strides. Normal riding can aim, with specific suppling exercises, to loosen the hips. But manual stretching from the ground remains the best way to target this area.

How Do I Do This?

1. Stand alongside your horse's right hip facing toward the rear.

2. Bend over and lift his right hind leg, supporting it with your hand around his fetlock.

3. Lift the hoof slightly forward and straight up, flexing the leg to approximately 90 degrees. Hold here for 20 seconds.

4. Draw the hind leg forward toward the front legs until the horse's cannon bone is horizontal to the ground. Hold here for 20 seconds.

5. Return the leg to the flexed position in step 3. Then, supporting the horse with your hand near his hock on the inside, lift the leg out to the side away from the body.

6. Gently return the foot to the ground and repeat the stretches on the opposite hind leg.

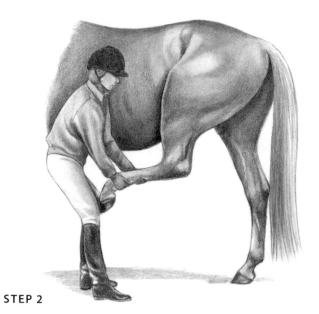

STEP 2

TIPS FOR SUCCESS: Some horses will require a few sessions to become comfortable with their hind legs being picked up and pulled in different directions. Before aiming for any stretching benefits in the first tries, give the horse time to become comfortable with what's being done with his body. Once trust and confidence are established, he will then benefit immensely more from stretching therapy.

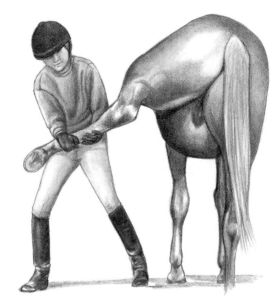

STEP 5

49. Shoulder Circles

The horse's front legs are secured to his trunk by a few important muscle groups and insertions. Many of the horse's muscles in his neck, pectorals, and abdomen work together. Any possible stiffness or compromise in one of these areas can greatly affect function of the horse's ribs and respiration, gait quality, use of his neck, and willingness to move forward. This stretch loosens the pectoral region and helps "open" the rib cage, allowing the horse to carry his trunk, and his rider, with greater ease and less weight on his forehand.

How Do I Do This?

1. Stand at your horse's shoulder facing toward the rear.

2. Bend over and lift his hoof off the ground, flexing the front leg slightly as you resume a standing position. Support his leg with your hand on the back of the leg slightly above his knee. Maintain a slight bend in that leg; be careful not to overflex the knee.

3. Gently push the foreleg across his body toward his other front leg.

4. Immediately draw it back outward toward you.

5. Push it back across his body.

6. Repeat this sequence four to six times with each leg.

TIPS FOR SUCCESS: Note that you are not *holding* the leg in any static position for a set period of time. This is a dynamic back-and-forth motion with the leg.

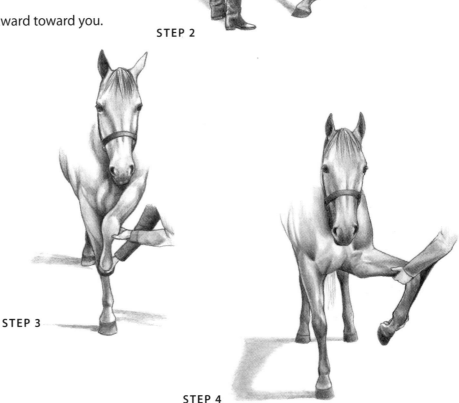

STEP 2

STEP 3

STEP 4

50. Bladder Meridian Exercise for Tension Release

Contributed by **Jim Masterson,** Former Equine Massage Therapist for the United States Equestrian Team

This simple but powerful exercise allows you to bypass the horse's survival-defense response and connect directly to that part of the horse's nervous system that is "guarding" tension. It shows you where the horse may be storing tension and helps him release it. It is important to go lightly and slowly. With this exercise, you are looking for the correlation between your touch and the horse's behavior or response to it. Often you will see that as you soften your touch, the horse's eyes soften immediately and he relaxes.

How Do I Do This?

1. Stand at the horse's head on the left side.

2. Place the flats of your fingertips or cup the palm of your hand on the poll just behind the left ear.

3. Barely touching the surface of the skin, *slowly* (it should take about a minute to run your hand from the poll to the withers) run your hand down the bladder meridian.

4. As you move your hand/fingers down the meridian, watch closely for subtle signs or responses to your touch from the horse. These include eye blinking and lip twitching. Larger responses that indicate a release of tension are licking, yawning, shaking the head, and snorting or sneezing repeatedly.

5. As your hand or fingers pass over a spot that causes the horse to blink, stop. Rest your hand/fingers on that spot, keeping your hand *soft* and the pressure *light*. Stay on that spot, watching the horse's responses. This may take just a second, or up to a minute. Be patient.

6. When the horse shows the larger responses of release — licking and chewing, yawning, shaking the head, or snorting or sneezing repeatedly — continue down the meridian using the above steps.

7. Repeat on the right side.

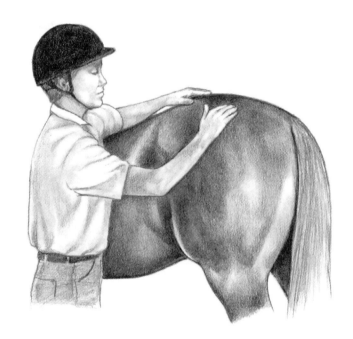

TIPS FOR SUCCESS: Horses lick, chew, yawn, blink, and twitch all the time. Look for the connection between your touch and the horse's behavior. (If you're not sure that the horse has blinked at a spot in response to your touch, put your hand a few inches before that spot and slowly go over it again. If he blinks on the same spot, it's a response.)

You can either repeat the exercise on the other side immediately or make sure to start on the other side the next time.

start

The bladder meridian is one of the major acupuncture meridians, running down each side of the body about 2 to 3 inches (5–8 cm) from the topline of the horse. This exercise begins at the poll, just behind the ear, and follows this meridian down the neck and back until it reaches the croup. From there it runs over the rump toward the "poverty groove," following this groove down the hind leg and over the side of the hock, cannon bone, and side of the fetlock to its termination on the coronary band.

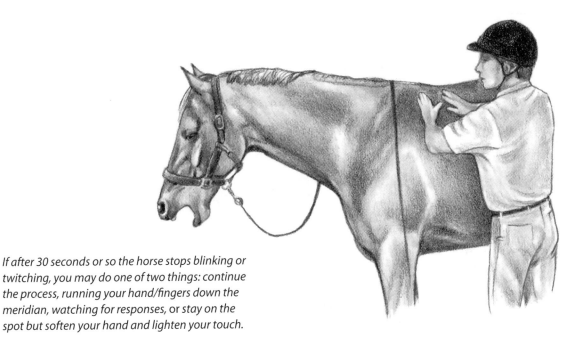

If after 30 seconds or so the horse stops blinking or twitching, you may do one of two things: continue the process, running your hand/fingers down the meridian, watching for responses, or stay on the spot but soften your hand and lighten your touch.

EXERCISE ROUTINES

Achieving fitness includes a number of aspects: strengthening soft tissue, increasing lung capacity, adapting the horse to metabolic stress, and loosening his joints and muscles. All this takes time and is accomplished in a cumulative way. Doing the following routines will not give you the results you may wish for in 1 week, but performed consistently over 2 or 3 months, they will bring the horse's *whole system* into better fitness.

FITNESS TRAINING

If you are just starting out, ride one of these complete routines every time you saddle up for a month or so, then intersperse them into your other schooling and training work. If your horse already has a baseline of fitness, use the exercises in these routines at the ends of your warm-ups and cooldowns. Just be sure to do every recommended exercise for each routine.

Fitness Routine 1

20. Tail Pull
10. Rein-Back up a Hill
19. Arena Interval Training
39. Lifting the Hind Legs
44. Shoulder Rotation Stretch
46. Pelvis Tucks

Fitness Routine 2

40. Bringing the Hind Legs Forward
45. Rear-Leg Circles
7. Loops and Poles
30. Horizontal Frame Conditioning
23. Shoulder Release Down and Back
20. Tail Pull

Fitness Routine 3

6. Temporomandibular Joint (TMJ) Massage
41. Stepping Over Slowly
25. Loosening the Back
38. Pick-up Sticks
31. Changing Speeds
48. Hip Stretch

Fitness Routine 4

44. Shoulder Rotation Stretch
47. Poll Stretch
18. Double Longe
26. Warm-up 1 — The Oval
12. Turn on the Forehand in Motion
24. Shoulder Release Down and Forward

MAINTAINING FITNESS

Moderately fit horses "detrain" or lose fitness within 2 weeks of exercise levels dropping off. Detraining can also occur when horses spend long periods of time schooling for a particular discipline and not executing enough aerobic exercise. So, no matter what discipline you school for on a daily basis, including trail riding, do your horse a favor and designate *at least* 1 day per week for riding one of the following routines.

Maintenance Routine 1

46. Pelvis Tucks
21. Tail Rotations
13. Exercise on a Slope
11. Rein-Back on a Curve
8. Waltzing with Your Horse (in hand)
22. Lateral Cervical Flexion

Maintenance Routine 2

47. Poll Stretch
45. Rear-Leg Circles
27. Warm-up 2 — Simple Trot Pattern
37. Trotting Poles in an Arc
2. Sprint Lines
49. Shoulder Circles

Maintenance Routine 3

23. Shoulder Release Down and Back
25. Loosening the Back
36. Striding In, Striding Out
9. Gearing Up to Gallop
32./33. Counter Canter (either variation)
42. Cantering on Uneven Terrain

Maintenance Routine 4

48. Hip Stretch
20. Tail Pull
16. Gymnastic Jumping
14. Riding a Drop
11. Rein-Back on a Curve
47. Poll Stretch

GOING FOR THE GOLD

These routines are intended to take a well-conditioned horse beyond a baseline of fitness. Combine and repeat the exercises in each routine at your discretion to create a 90-minute workout that includes three to five brief walk rests of 1 to 3 minutes each. You should aim to do two of these complete routines per week, adding your own preferred warm-up and cooldown.

The endurance, combined with the short bursts of intensity, in these routines better enables a horse's body to respond to athletic demands and increases his power. It can also reduce the risk of injury.

Gold Routine 1

22. Lateral Cervical Flexion
13. Exercise on a Slope
16. Gymnastic Jumping variation
19. Arena Interval Training
10. Rein-Back up a Hill
46. Pelvis Tucks

Gold Routine 2

25. Loosening the Back
34. Shoulder-In Repetitions
 2. Sprint Lines
37. Trotting Poles in an Arc
42. Cantering on Uneven Terrain
 3. Strengthening the Front End

Gold Routine 3

37. Trotting Poles in an Arc
16. Gymnastic Jumping
34. Shoulder-In Repetitions
32./33. Counter Canter (either variation)
15. Canter to Walk Downhill
11. Rein-Back on a Curve

Gold Routine 4

13. Exercise on a Slope
10. Rein-Back up a Hill (mounted)
15. Canter to Walk Downhill
 3. Strengthening the Front End
14. Riding a Drop
46. Pelvis Tucks

REHAB OR INJURY PREVENTION

The following routines are designed to provide a complete workout program for horses that have limited work ability or are recovering from injury. They blend muscle coordination exercises with basic fitness calisthenics. Begin by performing each routine once a week (aiming to do at least three routines per week).

After a few weeks, you can treat each routine as a "set," performing the exercises in any order you wish, and then starting from the top and working your way through the same order of exercises again. Do this three or four times in the same session. Eventually, you will learn to shuffle around the exercises in your "set" in the best way possible for you and your horse.

Rehab Routine 1

 4. Legging Up
46. Pelvis Tucks
21. Tail Rotations
10. Rein-Back up a Hill
11. Rein-Back on a Curve
23. Shoulder Release Down and Back

Rehab Routine 2

48. Hip Stretch
25. Loosening the Back
39. Lifting the Hind Legs
40. Bringing the Hind Legs Forward
41. Stepping Over Slowly
47. Poll Stretch

Rehab Routine 3

 6. Temporomandibular Joint (TMJ) Massage
 5. Transitioning Downward
13. Exercise on a Slope (walk only)
41. Stepping Over Slowly
 4. Legging Up
21. Tail Rotations

Rehab Routine 4

25. Loosening the Back
10. Rein-Back up a Hill
12. Turn on the Forehand in Motion
38. Pick-up Sticks
 1. Spiraling In and Out (walk only)
46. Pelvis Tucks

FOUR FITNESS GOALS

Equine fitness breaks down into roughly four areas: cardio, strength, balance, and suppleness. With those four areas accounted for, a horse in good health will reach his full performance potential no matter the discipline. This also means he will be easier and more fun to ride! Use the following list to create your own individualized workouts to target these four areas. A few exercises show up under more than one category because they are dual-purpose exercises (for example: promoting both strength and suppleness).

CARDIO FITNESS

Include two or three of these exercises per week, either on their own or as part of a longer session. Once your horse has achieved a good base of cardio fitness (generally after 3 months of consistent riding and exercise) you will only need to focus on maintenance.

Many of the following exercises can be interspersed into your normally planned riding session by setting aside 15 to 20 minutes to perform a couple of these patterns. Be sure to get your horse's heart and respiration elevated; otherwise, you are not pushing him enough to maintain his fitness level and he may lose condition.

2. Sprint Lines
9. Gearing Up to Gallop
13. Exercise on a Slope
16. Gymnastic Jumping
17. Sets and Reps for Arena
18. Double Longe
19. Arena Interval Training
26. Warm-up 1 — The Oval
30. Horizontal Frame Conditioning
31. Changing Speeds
37. Trotting Poles in an Arc
43. In and Out Leg-Yielding

STRENGTH TRAINING

Work on one or two of these exercises once or twice a week. Ideally, you should ride them on a day that you are not also taxing your horse's hindquarters in your normal riding. For instance, if you are a dressage rider and you've already ridden a lot of shoulder-ins or transitions, don't do the shoulder-in exercises. Save it for a riding day when you are focusing mostly on looseness or refreshing the basics in your riding.

Also, try not to get attached to only a few exercises — work your way through the whole list regularly. Each exercise asks different things of the horse's body.

2. Sprint Lines
4. Legging Up
8. Waltzing with Your Horse
10. Rein-Back up a Hill
11. Rein-Back on a Curve
14. Riding a Drop
15. Canter to Walk Downhill
20. Tail Pull
32. Counter Canter Loops
33. Counter Canter Serpentines
34. Shoulder-In Repetitions
36. Striding In, Striding Out
37. Trotting Poles in an Arc
39. Lifting the Hind Legs
41. Stepping Over Slowly
42. Cantering on Uneven Terrain
46. Pelvis Tucks

BALANCE AND ALIGNMENT

Perform two or three of these exercises daily, for at least 5 minutes in each direction. You do not need to drill the exercise repeatedly — just sprinkle them into your workouts to keep your horse's balance fine-tuned. Think about doing a Poll Stretch, for instance, when you're at the mounting block ready to get on your horse. Or do a modified version of Pick-up Sticks in a woodsy patch of trees on your way to the arena.

1. Spiraling In and Out
3. Strengthening the Front End
5. Transitioning Downward
7. Loops and Poles
12. Turn on the Forehand in Motion
13. Exercise on a Slope
18. Double Longe
22. Lateral Cervical Flexion
23. Shoulder Release Down and Back
24. Shoulder Release Down and Forward
28. Shoulder-In to Shallow Serpentine
32. Counter Canter Loops
33. Counter Canter Serpentines
36. Striding In, Striding Out
38. Pick-up Sticks
40. Bringing the Hind Legs Forward
42. Cantering on Uneven Terrain
47. Poll Stretch

SUPPLENESS AND FLEXIBILITY

Incorporate a couple of these exercises daily, either before or after your workout. Or you can use several of them together to serve as an entire workout. Once you get in the habit of blending these stretches into your daily handling of your horse, it will become second nature.

For example, I back my mare up a hill for eight strides when leading her from the paddock to the barn before I saddle her up. Then before I groom her, I do Shoulder Circles. Then, I brush her and put on the saddle, followed by Tail Rotations. Voilà! We've just done our calisthenics and now I don't need to think about them.

1. Spiraling In and Out
6. Temporomandibular Joint (TMJ) Massage
8. Waltzing with Your Horse (in hand)
10. Rein-Back up a Hill
12. Turn on the Forehand in Motion
21. Tail Rotations
25. Loosening the Back
27. Warm-up 2 — Simple Trot Pattern
29. Canter on the Honor System
35. Shoulder-In Traveling Out
44. Shoulder Rotation Stretch
45. Rear-Leg Circles
47. Poll Stretch
48. Hip Stretch
49. Shoulder Circles
50. Bladder Meridian Exercise for Tension Release

HOW TO USE THE PULLOUT EXERCISE CARDS

The cards in the back of this book are designed to be removed from the book and separated so that they serve as a convenient take-along reference. Each card is numbered and most cards contain a single exercise. Because it has several variations, exercise 17, Sets and Reps for Arena, takes up two cards.

Note: The following exercises share a card:

20. Tail Pull and 21. Tail Rotations

26. Warm-up 1 and 27. Warm-up 2

37. Trotting Poles in an Arc and 38. Pick-up Sticks

Once you have separated the cards, you can use them to follow the routines outlined on pages 126–27 or to create your own fitness and strengthening routines. Here are some suggestions for keeping your cards handy:

- Laminate them for longer wear.
- Punch a hole in the upper left-hand corners and keep the ones you're using at any given time on a binder ring or small carabiner.
- Collect them in a ziplock bag or plastic sandwich box.

If you lose a card or need a replacement set, visit *www.storey.com* to find a downloadable PDF.

GLOSSARY

anthropomorphism. Attributing human characteristics to nonhumans.

asymmetry. Lack of balance or symmetry.

balk. Refusal to move.

carpus joint. A movable joint (knee) that contains three joints and multiple bones.

cavesson. A kind of noseband used in training horses.

cervical. Of or relating to the neck.

coffin bone. The bottommost bone in the leg encased by the hoof capsule.

compression. In massage, pressing into the muscle and rotating the hand.

conformation. The correctness of a horse's bone structure, musculature, and its body proportions in relation to each other.

counter canter. Intentionally cantering on the wrong lead.

crest. The topline of the neck.

cribbing. The act of a horse gripping an edge such as a fence or stall door with his front teeth, arching his neck, and swallowing air.

dry muscles. Muscles that lack pliability.

effleurage. A soothing, stroking movement with an open, flat hand.

electrolytes. The "salt" molecules or minerals normally found in the bloodstream, including sodium, potassium, calcium, and magnesium. These elements are essential to maintaining a horse's normal body functions, and they can be critical when the horse is extremely active, under stress, or dehydrated. You can address an electrolyte imbalance by feeding your horse powdered electrolyte mixes or pastes, but it's wise to first consult your veterinarian.

extensor muscles. Any muscle that opens a joint, thereby increasing the angle between components of a limb.

fading. Early fatigue in an exercise session from working with too much tension.

fast-twitch muscles. Fast-twitch muscle fibers are characterized by a fast contraction speed. There are two categories of fast-twitch fibers; those that have a high capability to use oxygen and those that cannot use oxygen to a large extent. These are sometimes called intermediate and white fibers, respectively. Intermediate fibers are capable of using fatty acids as a fuel source and also utilize glycogen to a greater extent than do red fibers (slow-twitch muscles). White fibers use glycogen as their primary fuel source and do not use fatty acids to a great degree. Fast-twitch fibers are best suited to high-intensity exercise of a relatively short duration such as a 440-yard sprint up to a 2-mile race.

flexible. Pliable, elastic, or supple.

flexion. Bending a joint or limb.

glucose. A monosaccharide sugar. It is the principal circulating sugar in the blood and the major energy source of the body.

glycogen. A polysaccharide that is the main form of carbohydrate storage in animals and occurs primarily in the liver and muscle tissues. It is readily converted to glucose as needed to satisfy the body's energy needs.

gymnasticize. To work on a horse's strength and suppleness by using lateral work, transitions, and so on.

hock. The tarsal joint; corresponds to the ankle of the human foot.

horizontal frame. Having the poll and withers at the same height with the neck horizontal to the ground.

interval training. A short burst of speed that increases the heart rate, followed by a brief rest period during which the heart rate is kept at working level.

lactic acid. A syrupy, water-soluble liquid produced in muscles as a result of anaerobic glucose metabolism.

legging up. The practice of walking a horse on hard ground either in hand or under saddle.

leg-yield. A lateral movement in which the horse travels sideways and forward at the same time.

light seat. A seat that is halfway between a full balanced seat (in which most of the rider's weight is on the seat bones) and a two-point seat (in which the rider's entire seat is off the saddle, with only the inner thighs in contact with the saddle). A light seat allows the rider to change from a driving seat in full contact to a two-point seat easily while jumping a course of fences, and it allows the horse to move forward naturally as well.

longe/longeing. A technique for training horses where a horse is asked to work at the end of a longe line and respond to commands from a handler on the ground who is holding the line.

mandible. A lower jaw consisting of a single bone or of completely fused bones.

mitochondria. The energy factories in muscle cells.

musculoskeletal system. The system of body structures that provides energy and movement; the muscles, bones, and connective tissues of the body are grouped together into one system.

nuchal ligament. A band at the back of the neck, extending cranially from the occipital bone to the rear border of the great foramen and caudally to the seventh cervical spinous process.

poll. The junction of the vertebrae with the skull; an area of great sensitivity and flexion.

proprioception. A sense that uses cues from the inner ear and from receptors in the muscles, tendons, and joints to convey to the brain how the body is moving and where it is located in space.

quadriceps. A muscle of the thigh that extends the leg.

rein-back. Asking the horse to step backward; useful in training the equine athlete because it utilizes the horse's entire musculature.

ring of muscles. Muscles that include the abdominal, scalenus, and semiteninosus from the neck to the loin area.

sacrum. A set of sacral vertebrae at the end of the back.

scapula. Shoulder bone.

senior horse. A horse at or after about age 15 years.

serpentine. Motion of winding in and out of or around objects; serpentlike movement.

shoulder girdle. A group of large muscles including the trapezius, rhomboideus, latissimus dorsi, brachiocephalic, pectorals, and serratus ventralis muscles. Together they encircle the chest to attach and support the forelegs. In the horse there is no bony connection (joint) of the scapula to the trunk of the body, so these muscles are extremely important and strong. They help to absorb concussion forces traveling up the leg, and reduce impact on the spinal column.

shoulder-in. A lateral movement that many horsemen believe is one of the most important suppling movements available to riders. This movement can be done anywhere, but it's easiest to understand if you imagine it being done on the rail in an arena. The horse's forehand comes off the rail about 30 degrees, which puts the forehand and hindquarters on separate but parallel tracks. This movement is distinguished from the leg-yield because the horse is bent toward the direction he is moving, whereas in a leg-yield his body is bent away.

slow-twitch muscles. Slow-twitch muscle fibers are fibers characterized by a slow contraction speed and a high ability to utilize oxygen. They store a large amount of fatty acids as their primary fuel source. They are sometimes referred to as red fibers. These fibers are best suited for exercise of low intensity and long duration such as a 50-mile competitive trail ride.

spinous processes. Bony projections along each vertebra in the horse's spine. These projections are connected by a thick ligament called the "supraspinous ligament," which becomes the nuchal ligament from the withers forward.

stifle. At the front of the hind leg, just around and below the conjunction of skin to the abdomen on a healthy-weight horse; similar to the human knee.

supple. Capable of being bent or folded without creases, cracks, or breaks.

surcingle. A wide strap with rings that fastens around the barrel; side reins can be attached to the rings or driving reins can be run through them.

symmetry. The proper or due proportion of the parts of a body or whole to one another with regard to size and form; excellence of proportion.

telescoping (neck). When the horse extends his neck outward, vertebra by vertebra, like a retractable telescope.

temporomandibular joint (TMJ). Located at the upper rear of the lower jaw. This is the point where the jaw hinges in the skull.

topline. The outline of the top of the body.

transitioning downward. Gradual and smooth gait change to a slower tempo.

trapezius. A muscle that originates along the dorsal side of the neck near the poll, and inserts on the spine of the scapula.

withers. The highest point on the back on the ridge between the shoulder blades.

CONTRIBUTOR BIOGRAPHIES

With many thanks to the following people who generously shared some of their favorite exercises for our readers.

DR. SHERRY L. ACKERMAN, the author of *Dressage in the Fourth Dimension*, gives workshops based on its material. She is a popular clinician who is nationally known for integrating dressage theory and technique. For more information, visit *www.dressageinthefourth.com.*

YVONNE BARTEAU is an FEI trainer, rider, and instructor and a United States Dressage Federation (USDF) bronze, silver, and gold medalist. With a primary interest in competition dressage, Yvonne's training program is geared toward horses and riders who can work to high competitive standards both locally and nationally. She is the author of *Ride the Right Horse.*

JENNIFER BRYANT is the editor of *USDF Connection,* the member magazine of the United States Dressage Federation. A USDF bronze and silver medalist, she is the author of *The USDF Guide to Dressage, Olympic Equestrian: A Century of International Horse Sport,* and co-author of *A Gymnastic Riding System Using Mind, Body & Spirit.*

BECKY HART, a three time World Champion, was inducted into the American Endurance Ride Conference Hall of Fame in 1990, the same year she was named a Hertz/USET Equestrian of the Year and Overall Horseman of the Year by *Chronicle of the Horse.* With over 20,000 competitive miles in the saddle, she coaches for international competitions and has given sold-out appearances at Equine Affaire in Ohio and at Equitana in Louisville, Kentucky.

DR. JESSICA JAHIEL is an award-winning writer and internationally acclaimed lecturer and clinician. She answers questions in her e-mail newsletter, *Horse-Sense (www.horse-sense.org),* and writes for numerous publications including *Dressage Today, Equus,* and *Horse and Rider.* She is the author of a number of books on riding and training.

DAVID LICHMAN is a Five Star Parelli instructor, teaching students from Vancouver to Virginia and from Hawaii to Heidelberg. In 1991 he won a World Grand Championship on a Lite-shod Tennessee Walker Pleasure Horse. He has produced several books and DVDs pertaining to training gaited horses.

JIM MASTERSON, founder of the Masterson Method of equine therapy, regularly treats U.S. and international competitors at the World Equestrian Games and Pan American Games for endurance, the Nation's Cup for show jumping, and the World Cup for combined driving. His therapy finds and releases accumulated muscle and structural stress in key junctions of the horse's body that most affect performance. Visit *www.mastersonmethod.com* for more information.

MANOLO MENDEZ has trained dressage horses to Haute Ecole level since his early teens. He was second in charge at the famous Royal School of Equestrian Art (the Spanish Riding School) in Jerez, Spain during its early years. He and his students have given many exhibitions throughout Europe and Australia. He travels frequently to the United States for clinics.

GINA MILES has logged an impressive number of eventing victories in recent years, including winning the 2006 USEA Gold Cup, earning individual bronze and team gold at the 2007 Pan American Games, and clinching an individual silver medal at the 2008 Beijing Olympics. Her streak began in 2002 when she represented the United States at the World Equestrian Games.

MARK SCHUERMAN has trained riders and horses from beginning through national championship levels for 30 years, combining a Western style of horsemanship with solid dressage principles. He was pivotal in launching and growing the popular Arabian Sport Horse competitions that focus on the disciplines of dressage and flat classes for performance horses. Most recently, he has trained horses for international levels of endurance racing.

BETSY STEINER, author of *A Gymnastic Training System Using the Mind, Body, Spirit Approach,* has occupied the top ranks of dressage riders for over 30 years since her first Grand Prix success at just 20 years old. She has written numerous articles for top equestrian periodicals including *Practical Horseman* and *Dressage Today.* She is the creator of *EQUILATES,* a sport-specific Pilates-based exercise and body awareness program for equestrians.

RESOURCES

Websites

American Endurance Ride Conference
www.aerc.org

Association for the Advancement of Natural Horse Care Practices
www.aanhcp.net
Resource for humane care of equines

Barefoot for Soundness
www.barefoothorse.com
Hoof resource

Equi-analytical Laboratories
www.equi-analytical.com
Hay analysis

Equine Mechanics
www.equinemechanics.com
Biomechanics resource

Equine Studies Institute
www.equinestudies.org

EquiSearch.com
www.equisearch.com
All-around equine information from training to health issues

The Horse's Hoof
www.thehorseshoof.com
Barefoot hoof resource

World Conformation Horse Association
www.conformationhorse.com
Resource for conformation horse enthusiasts

Books

Briggs, Karen. *Understanding Equine Nutrition.* Lexington, KY: Eclipse Press, 2007.

Clayton, Hilary. *Conditioning Sport Horses.* Mason, MI: Sport Horse Publications, 1991.

Denoix, Jean-Marie, and Jean-Pierre Pailloux. *Physical Therapy and Massage for the Horse.* North Pomfret, VT: Trafalgar Square Publishing, 2005.

Heuschmann, Gerd. *Tug of War: Classical Versus "Modern" Dressage.* North Pomfret, VT: Trafalgar Square Books, 2007.

Hourdebaight, Jean-Pierre. *Fitness Evaluation of the Horse.* Hoboken, NJ: Wiley Publishing, 2008.

Meagher, Jack. *Beating Muscle Injuries for Horses.* Hamilton, MA: Hamilton Horse Associates, 1985.

Parsons, Heather Scott. *Care and Management of the Older Horse.* North Pomfret, VT: Trafalgar Square Publishing, 2002.

Paulo, Karen. *America's Long Distance Challenge: The Complete Guide to the Sport of Endurance and Competitive Trail Riding.* New York: Dutton, 1990.

Rachen-Schoneich, Gabriele, and Klaus Schoneich. *Straightening the Crooked Horse.* North Pomfret, VT: Trafalgar Square Publishing, 2007.

Steiner, Betsy. *A Gymnastic Riding System Using Mind, Body & Spirit.* North Pomfret, VT: Trafalgar Square Publishing, 2003.

Zidonis, Nancy, Amy Snow, and Marie Soderberg. *Equine Acupressure: A Working Manual.* Larkspur, CO: Tallgrass Publishers, 1999.

INDEX

Page numbers in *italics* refer to illustrations.

A

anatomy of head, neck, and spine, *49,* 49–50
Arena Interval Training, 68, *68*
arthritis, 27, *54*
assessing fitness, 17
attitude and behavior, 17

B

balance and alignment routines, 129
barefoot horses, 29
Bladder Meridian Exercise for Tension Release, 124–25, *124–25*
boarding facilities, limitations, 2
breathing patterns, 8–9
Bringing the Hind Legs Forward, 111, *111*

C

Canter on the Honor System, 86, *86*
Canter to Walk Downhill, 61, *61*
Cantering on Uneven Terrain, 113, *113*
cardio fitness, 17, 35–36, 128
Changing Speeds, 95, *95*
conditioning
    exercises, 37–46
    vs. schooling, 2, 31–32
cooling down, 71–72
    hosing off a horse, 72
coordination, 18
Counter Canter Loops, 97, *97*
Counter Canter Overview, 96, *96*
Counter Canter Serpentines, 98, *98*

D

diet, 3–4
Double Longe, 66–67, *66–67*

E

electrolytes, 3
energy level, 18
exercise
    cards, how to use, 129
    importance of consistency, 29
    requirements, 16
    routines, 126–27
Exercise on a Slope, 59, *59*
exercises
    conditioning, 37–46
    neck, 93–101
    stifle, 107–14
    strengthening, 55–68
    stretching, 117–25
    warm-up, 73–86

F

feeding, 3, 20
feet, healthy
    barefoot horse, 29
    hoof structure, 28, *28*
    proper alignment, 28–29
fitness
    achieving, 10–11, 13–14
    assessing, 17
    attitude and behavior, 17
    breaking your program into phases, 35–36
    cardio fitness, 17, 35–36, 128
    coordination, 18
    energy level, 18
    exercise requirements, 16
    general rules, 16–30
    getting a horse in shape, 19–21
    goals, 128–29
    importance of, 1–2
    maintenance, 24–25, 36, 126
    preparatory phase, 35
    rate of perceived exertion, 17
    recovery rate after workouts, 19
    strength-building phase, 36
    timeline, 34–35
    willingness, 17–18
five-year-old horse, *23*
    conditioning, 22, 24
footing for training workouts, 25
forage diet, 2–3
four-year-old horse, *23*
    conditioning, 22, 24
    tips, 24

G

Gearing Up to Gallop, 46, *46*
gold routines, 127
Gymnastic Jumping, 62–63, *62–63*

H

hay, 3
head and neck anatomy, 49, *49*
heart rate
    how to take a pulse, 19, *19*
    using a stethoscope, 19, *19*
Hip Stretch, 122, *122*
hoof structure and health, 28, *28–29*
Horizontal Frame Conditioning, 94, *94*

I

In and Out Leg-Yielding, 114, *114*
injury
    recovery routines, 127
    unexplained, 32–33

J

jaw, 33–34, *34*
    keeping your horse's jaw loose, 34
    Temporomandibular Joint (TMJ) Massage, 43
joint
    ligament noises, interpreting, 54
    pain, 8

L

lactic acid, 20
Lateral Cervical Flexion, 76–77, *76–77*
leg muscles, *6*
Legging Up, 41, *41*
Lifting the Hind Legs, 110, *110*
Loops and Poles, 44, *44*
Loosening the Back, 82, *82*

M

maintaining fitness, 36, 126
massage, 15, 115–116, *116*

Temporomandibular Joint (TMJ)
    Massage, 43
minerals, 3
movement, 2, 4, 30
    pointers for senior horses, 26
muscular system, 5–15
    good *vs.* bad muscle, *14,* 14–15
    healthy muscle tone, 11, *11, 13–14,*
        14–15
    leg muscles, 6
    neck muscles, 92, *92*
    one-sidedness, *14,* 14–15
    oxygen intake, 8–9
    ring of muscles, 47, 50–52
    shoulder muscles, 6, 7
    strengthening muscles, 9–10
    stretching, 15, 115
    structure, 7–8, *8*
    tightness and tension, 5–7, *6,* 9–11,
        13, 34
musculoskeletal system, 31–33, *33*

N

neck
    anatomy and stretching, *49,* 49–50
    determining correct position, 87–88,
        88
    exercises, 93–101
    musculature, 92, *92*
    range of motion, 88–89, *89*
    symmetry problems, 90–91, *90–91*
nutrition, 3–4

O

one-sidedness, *14,* 14–15
oxygen intake, 8–9

P

Pelvis Tucks, 120, *120*
Pick-up Sticks, 109, *109*
Poll Stretch, 121, *121*
posture, *47,* 47–52
    anatomy of good posture, *49,*
        49–50
    correct and incorrect, *48*
    ring of muscles, 49–52, *50–52*
    tense, *10*
    toned and relaxed, *11*
pulse, how to take a, 19

R

rate of perceived exertion, 17
Rear-Leg Circles, 119, *119*

recovery rate after workouts, 19
rehab routines, 127
Rein-Back on a Curve, 57, *57*
Rein-Back up a Hill, 56, *56*
rest days, 21
Riding a Drop, 60, *60*
ring of muscles, 47, 50–52
routines, 126–27
    create your own, 4

S

salt, 3
senior horse
    arthritis, 27
    conditioning pointers, 25–27
    dragging a lightweight object, 27
    maintaining fitness, 24–25
    movement, importance of, 26
    optimal exercises, 27
Sets and Reps for Arena, 64–65,
    64–65
sheath sounds, 54
Shoulder Circles, 123, *123*
shoulder muscles, *6, 7*
Shoulder Release Down and Back,
    78–79, *78–79*
Shoulder Release Down and Forward,
    80–81, *80–81*
Shoulder Rotation Stretch, 118, *118*
Shoulder-In Repetitions, 99, *99*
Shoulder-In to Shallow Serpentine, 85,
    85
Shoulder-In Traveling Out, 100, *100*
socializing, 2, 30
spine, anatomy, *49,* 49–50
Spiraling In and Out, 38, *38*
Sprint Lines, 39, *39*
Stepping Over Slowly, 112, *112*
stifle, 102–6
    assessing function, 103–4
    building strength, *104,* 104–6
    exercises, 107–114
    joint structure, 102, *102*
    tail carriage, 106
    weakness, 103
strength-building, 36, 47–54
    general exercises, 53–54
    specific exercises, 55–68
Strengthening the Front End, 40, *40*
stretching, 115
    exercises, 117–125
Striding In, Striding Out, 101, *101*
suppleness and flexibility routines, 129

sweat
    evaluating normal response, 18
    reading sweat patterns, 12, *12*
symmetry, *14,* 14–15
    problems, 90–91, *90–91*

T

tail carriage, 106
Tail Pull, 74, *74*
Tail Rotations, 75, *75*
telescoping gesture, 50
Temporomandibular Joint (TMJ)
    Massage, 43, *43*
tendons
    attachment to muscles, 7–8, *8*
    interplay with muscles, 6
tension, 5–7, *6,* 13
    jaw, 33–34
    posture, *10*
    vs. tone, 9–11, 13
three-year-old horse, *23*
    conditioning, 21–22
    tips, 22
timeline, 34–35
training plateaus, 31
training routines, 126
Transitioning Downward, 42, *42*
treats, 3
Trotting Poles in an Arc, 108, *108*
Turn on the Forehand in Motion, 58,
    58
turnout, 30

W

Waltzing with Your Horse, 45, *45*
Warm-up 1 — The Oval, 83, *83*
Warm-up 2 — Simple Trot Pattern,
    84, *84*
warming up, 30, 69–70
    exercises, 73–86
willingness, 17–18
workouts by age of horse, 21–27

Y

young horses
    conditioning and goals, 21
    diet, 4

ENHANCE YOUR EQUESTRIAN SKILLS
WITH MORE BOOKS FROM STOREY

101 Dressage Exercises for Horse & Rider by Jec Aristotle Ballou

Develop a firm foundation for your performance riding with these fully diagrammed standard dressage techniques. Basic beginner techniques to Olympian maneuvers will help you meet your goals for balance, straightness, rider position, and much more.

101 Jumping Exercises for Horse & Rider by Linda Allen & Dianna R. Dennis

This logical and consistent series of exercises includes easy-to-follow maps and instructions. It is a must-have workbook for beginning and experienced riders alike, as well as for trainers and instructors.

The Horse Behavior Problem Solver by Jessica Jahiel

This friendly question-and-answer sourcebook teaches you how to interpret and develop workable solutions to common horse behavioral problems. You'll learn how to break bad habits, handle a frightened horse, and much more.

How to Think Like a Horse by Cherry Hill

Detailed discussions illuminate how horses think, learn, respond to stimuli, and interpret human behavior. Explore everything that makes a horse tick — including their senses, pecking order, body language, and more — and gain a deeper understanding of the equine mind.

The Rider's Fitness Program by Dianna Robin Dennis, John J. McCully & Paul M. Juris

Build the strength, endurance, and skills you need to enhance your riding experience. This unique six-week workout routine includes more than 85 exercises explained through step-by-step photos — a perfect introduction for novice riders and a welcome refresher for seasoned equestrians.

Storey's Guide to Training Horses, 2nd Edition by Heather Smith Thomas

From start to finish, this is the definitive guide to developing a comprehensive, individualized training program for any type of horse, covering every aspect of handling, safety, training, and good horsemanship, both on and off the horse.

Join the conversation. Share your experience with this book, learn more about Storey Publishing's authors, and read original essays and book excerpts at storey.com. Look for our books wherever quality books are sold or call 800-441-5700.

1. Spiraling In and Out

1. Begin an active working trot rising on a big circle, 20 meters or larger.

2. After a few revolutions around the circle to ensure you are maintaining a steady and rhythmic trot, begin to shrink the circle down to as small as possible without losing tempo or balance.

3. With each stride, ask him to move over a little more until your circle gets smaller and smaller. You will most likely be on a circle about 10 or 12 meters in diameter.

4. After two revolutions around the small circle, begin to guide your horse one step at a time out to the larger circle you started on.

5. Repeat the exercise twice in each direction.

3. Strengthening the Front End

1. If you are not accustomed to riding your horse outside the arena, begin by *walking* him at a brisk pace on open terrain. Teach him to stay focused and marching along on all kinds of terrain.

2. Begin with a 1-mile (or 2 km) gallop but not on overly steep terrain. Rolling ground is fine, as are gentle slopes. Practice this once a week. If you have access to more mileage/land, you may want to ride a longer gallop every couple of weeks, up to 3 miles (5 km).

3. Maintain a gallop for a *sustained* period of time. Do not, for instance, gallop up a short hill and then break back to a trot. Short bursts will only excite the horse and do nothing to provide the continuous stress he needs to build strength. Allow the horse to settle into his gallop and maintain it.

2. Sprint Lines

1. Develop a nice working canter that is rhythmic and balanced.

2. As you approach the first cone, pick up an extended canter and sprint to the second cone.

3. Immediately after you pass the second cone, slow your horse down to your original working canter.

4. After passing the third cone, sprint forward to the fourth cone and return to the slower working canter at the fifth one.

5. Continue like this for 5 minutes, then take a 5-minute walk break and repeat the pattern for another 5 minutes.

6. Do this three times in each direction.

TIP FOR SUCCESS

- Pay attention to how your horse uses his body. Make sure he remains balanced and round with his ring of muscles.

4. Legging Up

1. Find an area that is mostly flat. Terrain with too much slope requires the horse to constantly adjust his stride. You want the horse to develop a steady rhythm and stride length.

   Pavement is desirable, but packed dirt ground works well too. Most boarding stables have a large parking area or roadway to suit the purpose.

2. Strive for a brisk, active walk with purpose where the horse is actively rolling his feet forward with each stride. Remember that you are trying to create a gentle concussion to lightly stress the horse's legs. To achieve this, the horse should travel at a lively pace. If riding, leave the horse on a loose rein, so he can carry his body in a relaxed and natural posture.

3. Walk for 1 or 2 miles (2–3 km), which equals about 12–20 minutes.

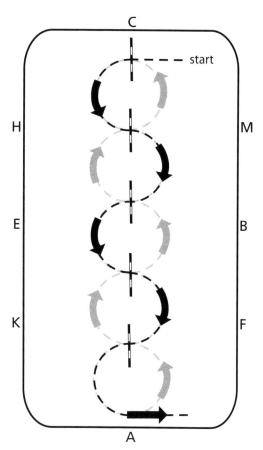

Each loop should be no larger than 10 meters, although you can adjust the size according to how your horse responds. Set up a single ground pole at the beginning of each loop on the serpentine.

TIPS FOR SUCCESS

- Don't sit down too early when riding from trot to walk.
- Continue posting until the very *last* stride of the trot so that your horse keeps his back lifted and round through the transition, rather than dropping it away from the rider's weight.

STEP 4

1. Face your horse, holding a short whip toward his inside barrel to invite him to bend.

2. Bending and rotating from the waist, position your shoulders the same way you would in the saddle, allowing the horse to mirror the movement.

3. There should be a sense of gently and carefully drawing the horse's shoulders toward your body. Be careful not to interrupt the rhythm of the walk.

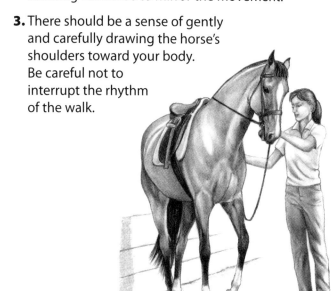

STEPS 2 & 3   STEP 4

STEP 5

9. Gearing Up to Gallop

Contributed by Yvonne Barteau

1. In an arena, develop a regular canter. Make sure you have a light rein contact and that the horse is in a rounded topline posture.

2. For 30 seconds, make the canter bigger (slightly faster and with longer strides).

3. Come back to a regular canter. Assess how well things went. Did your horse get excited? Did the horse change his stride with what felt like more propulsive power? Did you maintain a good contact?

4. Again make the canter bigger for 30 seconds and return to a regular canter.

5. Alternate 30-second bouts of bigger canter with 30 seconds of normal canter. Keep doing this for several minutes.

6. The next step is to stay in the bigger canter for longer than 30 seconds until it becomes a sustained period of galloping.

11. Rein-Back on a Curve

1. Designate a 10-meter circle using small cones or other markers.

2. Stand facing your horse, outside the cones.

3. Ask him to rein-back three straight strides to start.

4. Once you have that momentum, gently guide his shoulders slightly toward your left (away from you) and allow his hind end to swing to the right.

5. Continue walking him backwards around the 10-meter arc that you are now on.

6. If he loses the circle or gets stuck, you might need a long whip on the outside of his body to keep him on the circle.

7. Go halfway around the circle, then stop and praise him.

8. Finish the circle. Work your way up to being able to do the entire circle in one steady flow.

9. Repeat in the oppsite direction.

10. Rein-Back up a Hill

1. Find a gentle uphill slope with hard ground. A driveway will suffice.
   Stand your horse with his hind end facing up the hill.

2. Ask your horse to lower his head, ideally to shoulder level, before beginning to back up.

3. Ask for as many steps backwards as possible, aiming for 10 at the minimum. Maintain the rhythm of an ordinary walk — no faster, no slower.

4. Each day, add four more steps.

5. If your horse becomes crooked or braces his neck/head upwards, stop the movement.

Note: In the absence of a suitable hill, you can substitute a large pole for your horse to travel over backwards.

12. Turn on the Forehand in Motion

1. Ride in a walk with light contact and the horse in a good posture.

2. Gently half halt with your seat and back to downshift.

3. As soon as the horse responds, bend him to the right and push his hindquarters away from your right leg.

4. Keep asking him to step his right hind leg in front of his left hind leg.

5. Keep a little bit of forward momentum in your turn so that the horse's front feet keep marching in half steps forward instead of coming to a complete stop.

6. After you have executed a 180-degree change of direction, ride straight forward and resume the normal energy of the walk.

7. Repeat in the opposite direction.

TIPS FOR SUCCESS

- Watch to see whether your horse steps the same length backwards with each hind leg.
- If your horse shows signs of worry or braces himself into a bad posture when on the curved line, go back to rein-back on a straight line to relax him and restore symmetry.
- When you have mastered the above, back your horse around a figure eight with two 10-meter circles to incorporate both a curve in your rein-back and a change of direction.

TIPS FOR SUCCESS

- Because of his larger strides, the horse will need to use his back in a manner very different from his usual way of going: longer strides, a feeling of a bigger jump with each stride, and a swifter tempo.
- *Always* practice your 30-second bouts equally on both sides.

TIPS FOR SUCCESS

- The horse's front legs should remain in place and "mark time," that is, they should step up and down without moving forward.
- His hind legs should cross over, forming little X's with each stride.
- The exercise should be done in the same tempo and rhythm as if the horse were walking a straight line.
- If you feel, or have someone tell you, that your horse is dropping a hip, adjust the size of your turn and amount of bend until you are able to remedy the problem.

TIPS FOR SUCCESS

- If your horse tends to put himself in a bad posture and raise his neck or drop his back, perform this exercise unmounted. Use a gentle pressure on the halter or bridle to keep his neck low and use a crop aimed toward his chest to signal the rein-back.
- Do not ask for backward strides that are too long. Keep the movement rhythmic and balanced.

13. Exercise on a Slope

Find an area where the ground rises several feet on one side and slopes downward the same amount on the opposite side of a 20-meter circle. The footing must be somewhat smooth and stable.

1. Begin by longeing your horse at the walk to ensure he is managing his footwork on the uneven ground.

2. Once he is moving comfortably, pick up a trot around the circle. Keep the tempo slow.

3. Once your horse is trotting rhythmically around the circle, add a row of three or four ground poles to the bottom (downhill) side of the circle. They should be spaced appropriately for your horse to take only one trot stride between each one. The poles will encourage propulsion and a rhythmic stride.

4. Once your horse is negotiating the ground poles comfortably, add a small jump or cross-rail at the uppermost portion of the top (uphill) side of the circle. This way, the horse finishes his ascent with propulsion before rebalancing for the downhill section.

15. Canter to Walk Downhill

Contributed by Gina Miles

1. Warm up for 10 minutes with Cantering on Uneven Terrain (page 113), finishing at the top of the slope.

2. Proceed in a slow canter straight down a gentle grade.

3. Pick a midpoint on the downhill slope and transition into a walk.

4. Keep your horse straight in the transition; do not allow him to get crooked.

5. Walk the remainder of the slope.

6. Trot or canter to the top of the hill.

7. This time, divide the hill in thirds (if it is long enough), and at each third, transition from canter to walk. Then walk four strides and canter again to the next transition point.

8. Build up to being able to execute 10 of these transitions on each canter lead.

14. Riding a Drop

If you do not have a drop constructed at your barn, you can easily make one. You can construct one in a small area utilizing already-sloped ground, railroad ties, ditches, or whatever is handy. All that matters it that the horse has roughly a 2- to 3-foot (0.5–1 m) drop to jump into with stable ground on the opposite side to jump onto.

1. Approach the drop straight on at the walk, making sure that your horse is facing it straight and not crooked.

2. Just at the edge of the drop down, ask him to stop. Stand quietly for a few seconds to focus his attention on the drop.

3. From a standstill, ask him to step down into the drop. Keep your momentum going forward from this point, but not rushing. You want all four of his feet to step down in a balanced manner.

4. As soon as you are in the drop, urge him on with more energy. Ideally, he will jump his way out of the hole, rather than scrambling out.

5. Repeat three times.

16. Gymnastic Jumping

Place three trot poles on the ground approximately one trot stride apart. Then set up a cross-rail at a height of approximately 1 to 2 feet (0.3–0.6 m) spaced about 8 feet (2.5 m) away from the last trot pole.

1. Develop an active rising trot and trot *straight* over the *middle* of the trotting poles.

2. After crossing the last one, come into a half-seat or two-point position.

3. Go forward over the cross-rail.

4. Give your horse a short rest by trotting once around the edge of the entire arena.

5. Repeat for a total of 20 minutes, including rest periods.

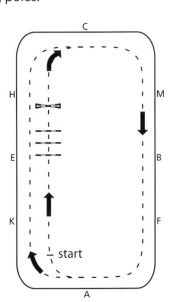

TIP FOR SUCCESS
- You can modify the exercise to a trot–halt format going downhill.

TIP FOR SUCCESS
- Keep the speed slow and easy enough for your horse to maintain the same rhythm all the way around the circle, rather than changing his rhythm from the uphill to the downhill portion.

VARIATION

1. Trot straight over the three ground poles and over the first cross-rail.

2. Immediately canter one stride straight ahead to the second cross-rail.

3. If you have trouble getting your horse into the canter before the second jump, space yourself more until your horse understands.

4. Rest him at the trot for 2 minutes around the edge of the arena before repeating.

TIPS FOR SUCCESS
- Sit with a tall but light seat.
- Maintain a steady non-rushing rhythm and hold a *straight* line.

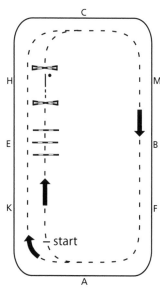

TIP FOR SUCCESS
- You may need to urge him more energetically and with a slightly forward seat if he does not respond by jumping out.

17. Sets and Reps for Arena

Contributed by Jennifer Bryant

To benefit even more from an arena workout, intersperse higher-intensity periods with brief breaks for your horse's muscles and mind. During the rest periods you can walk on a loose rein or let your horse stretch forward and down over his topline. Here's how to structure the workout.

- Perform the work set for 5 minutes.

- Allow your horse to rest for 5 minutes by stretching on a long rein at the walk or trotting easily in a stretched frame.

- Perform the work set for 4 minutes and rest for 4 minutes.

- Perform the work set for 3 minutes and rest for 3 minutes.

- Perform the work set for 2 minutes; final rest and cooldown.

Push yourself and your horse for a little more energy, good form, balance, etc., during each of the above four sets. The final 2-minute set should be almost perfect and really exerting.

18. Double Longe

Contributed by Mark Schuerman

1. Begin by lining up your horse to make a large circle to the left, then halt him and make him stand still.

2. Attach the inside line as shown in A. Keep a hand on this line for safety while attaching your outside line.

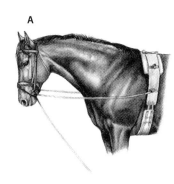

3. Attach the outside line as shown in B and run it behind his buttocks, just above his hock.

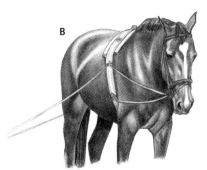

17. Sets and Reps for Arena (continued)

WORK SET B

1. In active working trot, go straight over a row of five raised (3-foot [0.9 m]) ground poles.

2. Pick up a canter and ride a shallow loop down long side and come back to the trot.

3. Turn down the centerline and leg-yield to the rail.

4. Canter halfway around the arena again.

5. Halt and rein-back eight steps.

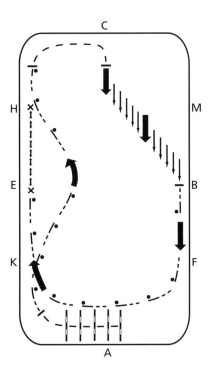

19. Arena Interval Training

1. Walk your horse briskly on a long rein for 5 to 10 minutes to warm up.

2. Canter at a moderate pace around the track of your arena for 2 full minutes.

3. Transition down and do a working trot for 2 minutes. This is your "rest" period.

4. Canter in the opposite direction for 2 minutes.

5. Repeat the canter-trot-canter sequence four times for a total of 24 minutes.

6. After the fourth set, bring your horse down to a walk. Let him walk at ease for a full 10 minutes until breathing and heart rate return to a resting rate.

An interval is a short burst of speed that increases the heart rate, followed by a brief rest period during which the horse's heart rate is kept at working level. Interval training will help improve or maintain your horse's overall cardiovascular fitness. If you want to increase, rather than maintain, fitness over time, gradually add a second work set after the long walk break.

4. When he is relaxed, lower his foot with your right hand, straighten his leg with your left hand, and ask him to put his foot down and back until it is flat on the ground. Feel for his shoulder blade (scapula) to drop slightly as he does this. Do not ask him to step back too far.

5. Allow the horse to release. The horse may stay in this position as long as he wants or he may go back to a normal stance.

6. Duplicate the exercise on the opposite side.

STEP 4

STEP 5

21. Tail Rotations

1. Stand close behind or slightly off to the side of your horse, behind his hip on one side.

2. Hold the dock of his tail (about 4 inches [10 cm] from the top of his tail) with both hands and lift gently straight up 2 to 4 inches (5–10 cm).

3. Make small circular motions with the tail, circling in each direction three to five rotations.

4. Be sure your circles are evenly sized in both directions of rotations. If not, it might be an indication of stiffness or tightness in the horse's back.

5. Move slowly in this stretch so the horse does not clamp his tail.

TIP FOR SUCCESS
- You can get your horse to relax by gently rubbing the hairless underside at the dock. Once he relaxes, move into the circling motion.

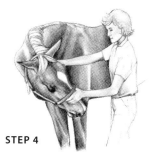

---

5. When he is relaxed, slide your right hand under the bulb of the heel and lower his foot to the ground, keeping your left hand on his shoulder. Feel for his shoulder blade (scapula) to drop slightly as he does this. Do not pull his leg out too far.

6. Step back and allow the horse to release. As he releases his leg down and forward, pick a spot on the ground close to the horse for him to put his foot. Do not continue to hold the foot out because he could fall forward or hyperextend the leg — not good!

7. Repeat this exercise on the opposite side.

STEP 5

STEP 6

3. Move your right hand 2 or 3 inches (5–7.5 cm) down the neck vertebrae. Keep your left hand on the nose.

4. Gently flex his head toward you with the left hand, pushing gently away with the right hand. Bring the nose toward the shoulder, stepping back as you go.

5. Relax both hands again and move the right hand farther down the vertebrae of the neck.

6. Bring the horse's nose farther back toward the shoulder each time until you have brought the head all the way back to the shoulder and your hand all the way down to the lower vertebrae of the neck. As the horse relaxes, gently rock the head and neck with both hands as you go.

7. Step back and allow the horse to release. Duplicate on the opposite side.

STEP 3   STEP 4

25. Loosening the Back

1. Set up five ground poles on flat ground spaced so that your horse can walk comfortably over them without taking a stride *between* any of them.

2. Before heading into the arena for your workout, ride over the poles.

3. Continue straight back and forth over them until you feel your horse's stride change; that is, he begins to keep a steady cadence over the poles and is reaching nicely with a long stride over the poles, beginning to round up his back under your seat, and stretching his neck toward the ground.

4. On some days, it may require several trips over the poles (up to 10 or more) until you notice a change; on other days, your horse may loosen up after crossing the poles only twice.

5. After you feel your horse's muscles becoming looser, establish your contact and head to the arena for your workout.

28. Shoulder-In to Shallow Serpentine

Contributed by Betsy Steiner

1. In an active trot, ride shoulder-in for the first third of your arena's long side (from the letters K–V).

2. "Peel" off the rail and ride to X.

3. At X, change your horse's bend to the left and ride back to the rail at H.

4. Once you return to the rail at H, ride a 10-meter circle to the right.

5. Proceed the rest of the way around the arena to repeat exercise again at K.

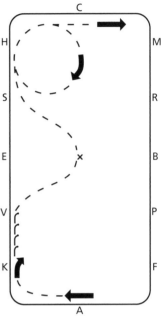

26. Warm-up 1 — The Oval

1. Visualize a giant oval around the edge of your arena.

2. On the long sides of your oval, ride a big ground-covering trot with lots of energy.

3. As you come to the rounded ends on the top and bottom of your oval, downshift to a slower trot.

4. As you come out of the rounded ends, immediately ask your horse to surge forward in a big, bold trot down the long side of the arena again.

5. Downshift again coming into the top/bottom of your oval. Continue this sequence for several minutes, in both directions.

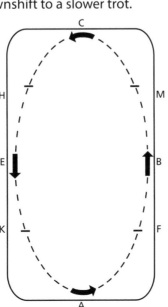

29. Canter on the Honor System

Contributed by Dr. Jessica Jahiel

1. Warm up thoroughly at the walk, and perhaps also (depending on your horse's fitness and flexibility) at the trot.

2. When warmed up, go into a light half-seat, lengthen your reins until they are *loose* rather than *long*, and allow/encourage your horse to canter on a large circle (at least 20 meters).

3. Continue cantering for at least 5 minutes and possibly much longer, depending on your horse's level of fitness.

Shoulder-In to a Diagonal in the Trot

Follow the above pattern through step 3, except once you peel off the rail, extend your horse's trot strides all the way across the arena to M. When you get to the rail at M, slow down a bit and reorganize his working trot.

TIPS FOR SUCCESS

- Keep a consistent rhythm throughout this pattern.
- Maintain an energetic trot to build strength.
- Work in both directions.

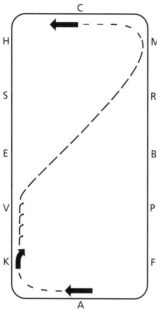

TIPS FOR SUCCESS

- Use this simple exercise to work on your seat. Sit deeply, *follow* the movement, keep your eyes *up*, and stretch your legs down from your hip.
- Keep your horse *straight* over the middle of the poles.
- Note any changes in the way he feels from day to day. Does he bump into the poles when you start? Is he distracted? Does his back seem sore and unwilling to round up? Is he resisting your aids to be straight?

EQUINE FITNESS
27. Warm-up 2 — Simple Trot Pattern

1. Begin in an energetic working trot to the right. Ride once around the edge of the arena, maintaining a steady rhythm.

2. At A, ride one 20-meter circle.

3. As soon as you leave the circle and are on a straight line again, ask your horse to increase his trot tempo to cover as much ground as possible.

4. At the opposite end of the arena, resume your steady working trot tempo. When you come around to A again, ride another 20-meter circle and repeat step 3.

5. Repeat this a few times and then do the same pattern in the canter.

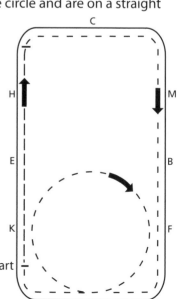

This exercise is pleasant for the horse but can be challenging for the rider. There is no use of reins and no sitting deep in the saddle — your contact and communication with the horse come from your legs, weight and balance, breathing, and voice.

30. Horizontal Frame Conditioning

1. Begin by trotting your horse in a "horizontal frame," meaning his poll and withers are at the same height and his neck is horizontal to the ground like a table.

2. When you feel he is reaching into the bit and you have good contact, begin to shorten the reins half an inch at a time.

3. Shorten the reins until the horse's poll is now the highest point on his body. Depending on his height, his ears might now be relatively level with your chest.

4. Keep the trot active and ride in this frame about 15 seconds.

5. Gradually let the reins slide through your fingers a half inch at a time until the horse is in a frame with his poll *lower* than his withers.

6. Ride 15 seconds in this frame.

7. Repeat the whole sequence several times in each direction.

8. When you are performing it well, also ride it at the canter.

31. Changing Speeds

1. Choose either a working trot or a working canter; this exercise is beneficial in only those two gaits.

2. Proceed in your working gait on either a very large circle or a straightaway.

3. Making sure your horse is in a good posture, extend your gait.

4. Remain in the extended pace at least as long as you were in the working gait. For example, if you ride three-quarters of the way around the arena in the working canter, extend the canter for the same distance.

5. Make a *gradual* downward transition to the working gait.

6. Repeat numerous times in both trot and canter in both directions. It is only effective when the horse is pushed enough to take more oxygen into his body.

32. Counter Canter Loops

1. Begin on the right lead. Execute a few large circles to establish a clear and consistent rhythm.

2. Leaving your circle, ride through the corner and then immediately peel off the rail toward the center of the arena.

3. When you are about 10 feet (3 m) from the rail, ride straight ahead for about 7 feet (2 m). Make sure your horse goes straight at this point.

4. Guide him back to the rail for your next corner.

5. Instead of doing another shallow loop right away, ride straight down the following long side of your arena.

6. Practice in both directions.

TIPS FOR SUCCESS
- If the horse changes his posture or his rhythm, make your loop even more shallow or "flatter" until you can ride it without fluctuations.
- Be precise with your geometry because the difference in loop sizes taxes your horse's postural muscles distinctly.

33. Counter Canter Serpentines

1. Develop a working canter on the right lead and begin by riding alternately between a 20-meter-diameter circle and a 15-meter-diameter circle, to get the horse on your aids for changing the size of his bend.

2. When you've established a consistent canter, ride the first loop in the diagram. Make sure your horse's rhythm, bend, and posture remain even throughout.

3. Ride straight down the following long side of the arena.

4. Play around with the different patterns, tracing each one with your horse and alternating between them.

5. Work in both directions.

TIP FOR SUCCESS
- Follow the suggested geometry precisely. The shape of the pattern determines whether or not the horse balances himself correctly.

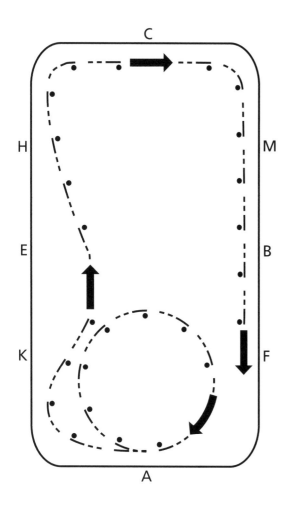

TIP FOR SUCCESS

- If while you are adjusting the reins, your horse becomes fidgety with the contact or drops it, stop at *exactly* that length of rein and ride forward until you regain his connection to your hand.

STEP 1

STEP 3

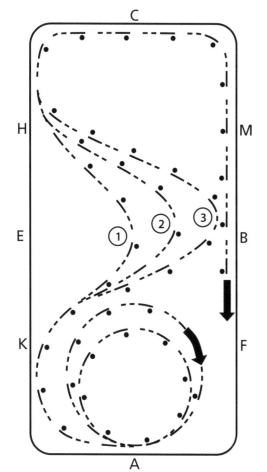

TIPS FOR SUCCESS

- Do not make the transitions too close together without the time to establish a clear rhythm in each pace. Be sure to maintain a good posture in the horse throughout the entire exercise.
- Allow the horse's neck to lengthen forward when you transition to the extended gait. If you do not, his body will remain blocked in the extension.

34. Shoulder-In Repetitions

1. In an arena or flat surface with good, level footing, begin in an active working trot traveling clockwise. Note your horse's heart rate on the heart monitor after 4 minutes.

2. Maintaining a steady rhythm, execute 10 steps of shoulder-in, taking note of the horse's heart rate as he moves over.

3. Note how many strides of shoulder-in it takes until his heart rate rises noticeably.

4. Once you have determined the number of strides in your set, continue trotting around the arena riding various simple patterns (big circles, diagonals, and figure eights). Every 60 seconds, execute a shoulder-in set.

5. After each set, continue riding simple patterns for 60 seconds.

6. Repeat this cycle for 5 to 10 minutes in both directions, depending on your horse's skill with shoulder-in. Keep checking the heart rate to ensure you are getting a consistent rise in heart rate for each shoulder-in set.

35. Shoulder-In Traveling Out

Contributed by Manolo Mendez

1. Begin in an active working trot traveling clockwise around your arena.

2. At one end of the arena, ride a 15-meter circle to maintain your rhythm and establish an inside bend.

3. Ride a quarter of the way again around the circle and then gently displace the horse's front end with your right leg in the direction of the rail. You should end up with a slight diagonal slant in the horse's body toward the rail.

4. Ask him to move sideways from your right leg toward that rail while ensuring that his forehand remains ahead of his haunches, as in the diagram.

5. As you travel slightly sideways to the rail, keep the horse's spine bent to the right. His body should feel "curled" around your right leg.

6. When you reach the rail, accelerate the trot for two or three strides to push the horse's hind legs back underneath him.

7. Travel around the entire arena and then repeat.

36. Striding In, Striding Out

Before you begin, set up eight ground poles according to the diagram. Place the first four poles spaced apart at a distance that is roughly 1 to 2 inches (2.5–5 cm) shorter than the length of your horse's normal stride in the trot. After this set of four poles, leave a 32.8-foot (10 m) gap and then set up four more poles, this time spacing the poles at a distance 1 to 2 inches (2.5–5 cm) longer than the length of your horse's normal stride.

1. Develop a brisk working trot.

2. Aim straight over the first set of four poles.

3. About 3 feet (1 m) before you reach the first pole, ask your horse to slow down a little and shorten his stride.

4. Proceed over the poles in just four strides. Your horse should not take any strides between the poles or try to cover two poles at once.

5. Proceed straight to the next set of poles and start to push his trot more actively forward.

6. Ride over the second set of poles visualizing an extended trot. Again, your horse should cover the poles in just four strides, no more and no less.

37. Trotting Poles in an Arc

1. Walk your horse over the ground poles to ensure that the spacing is correct for his stride. Remain on the arc of the circle while traversing exactly over the *middle* of each pole. Do not drift to the outside edge!

2. Once your horse is going well in the walk, ride the ground pole circle in the rising trot.

3. Repeat several times in each direction, keeping an active trot and maintaining an inside bend through your horse's neck and rib cage.

VARIATION

Ride the same pattern as above, except raise the poles 6 inches (15 cm) off the ground with jump standards or cones. Ride with a slightly forward and light seat.

TIP FOR SUCCESS
- Make a note if one direction of the exercise seems more difficult than the other. This indicates asymmetry in your horse's way of going, which you can address with targeted stretching after the session.

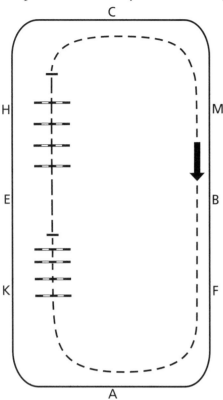

"Above normal" means 20 beats or more above his normal heart rate for a normal working trot. For most horses, it will take just four or five strides. That number of strides is the "set" that will be repeated throughout the workout.

EQUINE FITNESS

38. Pick-up Sticks

You will need a number (at least 10, but more is better) of ground poles or large-diameter PVC pipes, which are lighter and easier to handle. Scatter them around a 20-meter area so that some of them are lying across each other and others are away from the group in a random pattern.

1. Mount your horse and find a line from one side of the area to the other through that mess of poles.

2. For safety, walk the line first.

3. Once at the other side, turn around and find a different way back.

4. If you are finding success, then try jogging a few steps.

5. Find as many routes through the pole pile as possible, or make up little patterns.

TIP FOR SUCCESS
- Keep only a loose rein contact and, as much as possible, don't interfere with your horse. Point him where you want to go, sit back, and let him find his way. You are teaching him to balance himself.

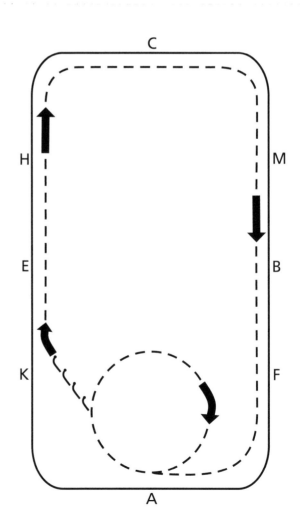

39. Lifting the Hind Legs

1. Position your horse so that he is standing squarely and quietly along a fence, with his weight evenly distributed over all four feet.

2. Ask your horse to relax his head and neck so that his back is rounded, not hollow. Ideally, have him lower his head so that his poll and withers are at the same height.

3. Keeping his neck stretched, reach back with your longe whip or a bamboo cane and gently tap his near hind leg until he raises that foot off the ground.

4. Change direction along the fence and repeat with the opposite hind leg.

5. Gradually progress to having him flex the leg and hold the foot in the air for up to 10 seconds (do this by gently tapping again when he tries to put the foot back down on the ground).

41. Stepping Over Slowly

1. Place a tall but relatively soft object on level ground (an arena is ideal, but a driveway will suffice).

2. Lead your horse straight up to the object and halt.

3. Ask him to step very slowly over the object, one foot at a time.

4. Once he picks up his hind leg to step over the object, try to make him hesitate a few seconds so that he prolongs the motion of clearing his leg over to the other side.

5. Repeat a few times back and forth.

40. Bringing the Hind Legs Forward

1. Position your horse so that he is standing squarely and quietly along a fence, with his weight evenly distributed over all four feet.

2. Ask him to lower his neck by using light downward pressure on his cavesson or reins.

3. Keeping your left hand near his nose/reins in case he tries to brace upward out of the posture, tickle just behind his girth area to ask him to engage his belly and round his back.

4. Now ask him to bring one hind foot forward under his body by gently tapping with your whip behind his cannon bone or on the inside of the leg.

5. Keep your horse stretching forward with his neck. Then ask each hind leg to keep inching forward under the body.

6. Once you have achieved the desired stance, ask him to stand quietly in this posture for 10 to 15 seconds and then allow him to simply be "at ease" before moving forward.

42. Cantering on Uneven Terrain

1. Warm up by walking your horse vigorously on a long rein out in the open space.

2. Pick up a canter on either lead and start by cantering the gentlest slopes at first, cutting across the downward grades at 45-degree angles.

3. Gradually make your approach to the downward grades steeper.

4. Keep the speed of the canter consistent regardless of the grade of the terrain. At first, you may need a few strong half halts to show your horse not to change speeds when the terrain changes.

5. Keep doing this exercise for as long as possible. Don't quit after a few times around your open space; horses, like humans, generally improve on the exercise after they've been at it a while, have figured out where to put their feet, and have allowed themselves to relax into the movement.

TIP FOR SUCCESS

▪ Do this exercise *as slowly as possible* to build strength in the stifle. Rushing over the obstacle will have no benefit.

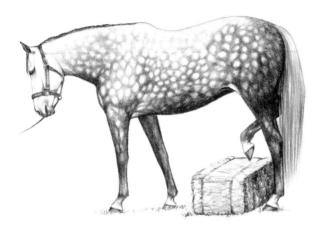

Use an object about 2-feet (0.6 m) high that will make your horse pull his leg up to walk over. It should be suitably soft in case he gets worried and steps on or kicks it. A hay bale works fine, as does a collapsible mesh laundry basket with some added weight to keep it in place.

TIP FOR SUCCESS

▪ Every horse responds differently to whip cues. Some horses will lift their hind legs when asked with a light touch near the middle of the cannon bone, but others will be more responsive to the area just below the hock or on the inside of their legs. Play around to see what works best for your horse and praise him whenever he even attempts to do what you're asking.

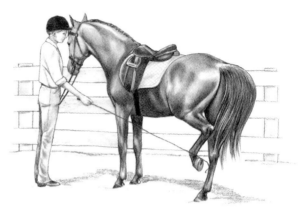

You can do this work with your horse outfitted in a plain halter, bridle, or longeing cavesson. You will need a longe whip or long bamboo cane.

TIPS FOR SUCCESS

▪ Posture is critical in this exercise. Maintain a light contact with the horse's mouth so that you can guide him back to a good frame if he tries to hollow out when losing his balance.

▪ Try to ride the horse in this exercise with your reins about 2 inches (5 cm) longer than for normal arena riding. His stretched-out neck will help keep his balance over the terrain.

When a horse uses his back and ring of muscles properly (above), he builds them stronger thanks to the added resistance of terrain changes. When he travels in a bad posture, on the other hand, the stress (jarring) of the exercise taxes his joints and tendons.

TIP FOR SUCCESS

▪ As always when dealing with your horse's balance, take time to develop the exercise day by day. Be satisfied with a little progress at a time and reward often.

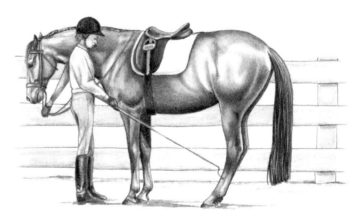

You will need a plain halter, bridle, or longeing cavesson, as well as a longe whip or long bamboo cane.

43. In and Out Leg-Yielding

Contributed by Becky Hart

1. Begin by riding with the group of riders in single file, trotting down an open section of roadway (or arena). Maintain a horse's length spacing between the horses.

2. When all the horses are sustaining the same speed, have the last horse in line leg-yield three steps to the left and immediately extend the trot to pass the other riders.

3. At the front of the line, slow down to regain the trotting tempo of the group.

4. Leg-yield three steps to the right to arrive back in the single-file line in lead position.

5. As soon as the first horse has established position back in the single-file line, the horse now at the end of the line repeats the sequence.

6. When the terrain is suitable, continue with this exercise for a couple of miles, or at least 15 minutes.

44. Shoulder Rotation Stretch

1. Stand facing your horse's shoulder.

2. Using both hands, clasp the leg above the knee and raise it just to the point of resistance, then release it slightly.

3. Gently rotate the leg three to five times in a 3-inch (8 cm) circle moving the leg forward and back, not side to side.

4. Increase the diameter of your circle to 4 or 5 inches (10–13 cm) and repeat three to five times.

5. Increase the diameter of your circle to 6 or 7 inches (15–18 cm) and repeat.

6. Reverse the direction of the rotation, starting with a small circle as described above and increasing the diameter every three to five rotations.

7. Return your horse's hoof to its original position and repeat the entire sequence two or three times.

8. Repeat the sequence on his other front leg.

45. Rear-Leg Circles

1. Stand near your horse's left hip, facing his tail.

2. Bend over and place your right hand around the inside of his leg above the hock. Place your left hand on the back side of his fetlock.

3. Lift the leg off the ground and pull it forward several inches and then set the toe on the ground for a count of 3 seconds.

4. Slowly pull the leg to the outside and touch the hoof to the ground for another 3 seconds.

5. Push the leg behind the horse and touch the hoof to the ground for 3 seconds.

6. Rest the leg in its original position before repeating the sequence.

7. Repeat twice with each hind leg.

46. Pelvis Tucks

1. Stand squarely behind your horse (make sure he knows you're there!).

2. Tuck the tips of each thumb just under the dock of his tail.

3. Extend your fingers straight up to form a "box" with your thumbs.

4. Apply direct pressure into the horse's buttocks muscle with the tips of your index fingers.

5. If the horse does not immediately tuck or "squat" his pelvis away from that pressure, try a light tickling or scratching motion.

6. Repeat at least twice.

TIP FOR SUCCESS

- Move slowly in this stretch. You do not want the horse to pull his leg up and away from you.

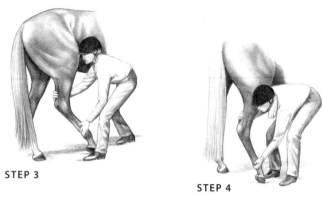

STEP 3

STEP 4

STEP 5

TIPS FOR SUCCESS

- Be sure the horses in the line maintain a steady rhythm rather than racing the passing horse to allow clear transitions. This extending and then reducing of pace is part of the exercise's value.
- Ride good-quality leg-yields, applying the aids correctly to get a decent bend in your horse's spine and sufficient crossover in the front and hind limbs.
- If necessary, do this exercise at a walk first to accustom the horses to the idea.

This exercise is most suited for riding in a small group on a dirt road or wide trail. It can be modified, however, to work for just two horses riding together. It can also be modified from use on the trail to use in the arena if necessary.

TIP FOR SUCCESS

- Some horses are very sensitive in this area and others are duller. You may need to alter your hand position to find your own horse's response.

STEP 2

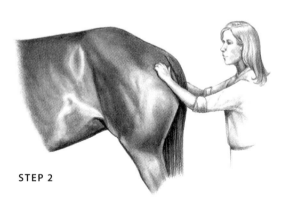

STEP 2

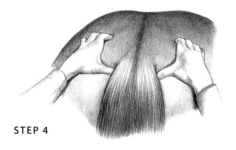

STEP 4

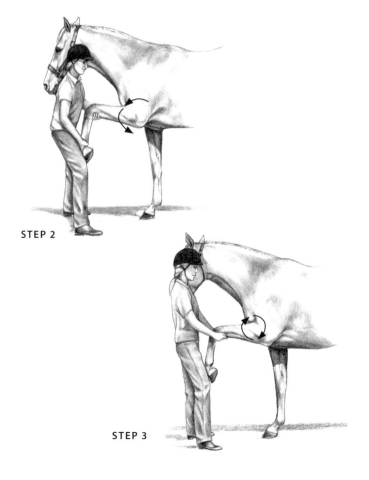

STEP 3

47. Poll Stretch

1. Stand alongside your horse just behind his jaw, facing forward.

2. Place your right hand on his neck just behind his poll and apply light pressure to prevent him from bending his neck toward you.

3. With your left hand, either hold the bridge of his nose or the halter nosepiece and draw just his head toward you. You want only his head to swivel toward you, while his neck remains straight. Be sure his ears and nostrils remain level. This indicates that he is not tipping his head, which you do not want.

4. Hold the stretch approximately 20 seconds then repeat on the other side.

48. Hip Stretch

1. Stand alongside your horse's hip facing toward the rear.

2. Bend over and lift his hind leg, supporting it with your hand around his fetlock.

3. Lift the hoof slightly forward and straight up, flexing the leg to approximately 90 degrees. Hold here for 20 seconds.

4. Draw the hind leg forward toward the front legs until the horse's cannon bone is horizontal to the ground. Hold here for 20 seconds.

5. Return the leg to the flexed position in step 3. Then, by supporting the horse with your hand near his hock on the inside, lift the leg out to the side away from the body.

6. Gently return the foot to the ground and repeat the stretches on the opposite hind leg.

49. Shoulder Circles

1. Stand at your horse's shoulder facing toward the rear.

2. Bend over and lift his hoof off the ground, flexing the front leg slightly as you resume a standing position. Support his leg with your hand on the back of the leg slightly above his knee. Maintain a slight bend in that leg; be careful not to overflex the knee.

3. Gently push the foreleg across his body toward his other front leg.

4. Immediately draw it back outward toward you.

5. Push it back across his body.

6. Repeat this sequence four to six times with each leg.

TIP FOR SUCCESS
- Do not *hold* the leg in any static position for a set period of time. This is a dynamic back-and-forth motion with the leg.

50. Bladder Meridian Exercise

Contributed by Jim Masterson

1. Stand at the horse's head on left side.

2. Place the flats of your fingertips or cup the palm of your hand on the poll just behind the left ear.

3. Barely touching the surface of the skin, *slowly* (it should take about a minute to run your hand from the poll to the withers) run your hand down the bladder meridian.

The bladder meridian runs down each side of the body about 2 to 3 inches (5–8 cm) from the topline of the horse. This exercise begins at the poll just behind the ear and follows this meridian down the neck and back until it reaches the croup. From there it runs over the rump toward the "poverty groove,"  *following this groove down the hind leg and over the side of the hock, cannon bone, and side of the fetlock to its termination on the coronary band.*

STEP 2

STEP 3

STEP 4

TIPS FOR SUCCESS

- If your horse has an old injury he may have inflammation in his poll and be resistant towards this stretch. Go easy at first and heed any adamant fussiness.
- If your horse is at all tight on one side of his poll or upper neck, you will see him react to the stretch by sighing, licking his lips or chewing, or closing his eyes sleepily. If you see this, repeat another stretch on that side.

Do not tilt the horse's nose like this. Keep his head straight.

4. As you move your hand/fingers down the meridian, watch closely for subtle signs or responses to your touch from the horse. These include eye blinking and lip twitching. Larger responses that indicate a release of tension are licking, yawning, shaking the head, and snorting or sneezing repeatedly.

5. As your hand or fingers pass over a spot that causes the horse to blink, stop. Rest your hand/fingers on that spot, keeping your hand *soft* and the pressure *light*. Stay on that spot, watching the horse's responses. This may take just a second, or up to a minute. Be patient.

6. When the horse shows the larger responses of release — licking and chewing, yawning, shaking the head, or snorting or sneezing repeatedly — continue down the meridian using the above steps.

7. Repeat on the horse's right side.

TIP FOR SUCCESS

- If after 30 seconds the horse stops blinking or twitching, you may do one of two things: continue the process, running your hand/fingers down the meridian, watching for responses, *or* stay on the spot but soften your hand and lighten your touch.

TIP FOR SUCCESS

- Give the horse time to become comfortable with what's being done with his body. Once trust and confidence are established, he will then benefit immensely more from stretching therapy.

STEP 2

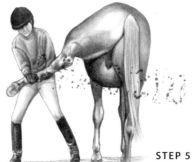

STEP 5